CHARLES N. GUTHRIE

my jump from heaven

MONTEZUMA
PUBLISHING

Published by
Montezuma Publishing
Aztec Shops Ltd.
San Diego State University
San Diego, California 92182-1701
619-594-7552
www.montezumapublishing.com

ISBN: 978-0-7442-9276-3

Publishing Manager: Kim Mazyck
Design and Formatting: Lia Dearborn
Cover Design: Lia Dearborn
Quality Control: Jasmine Baiz

Acknowledgments

Dorothy and Norris Guthrie who raised me with love.

The San Diego Police Department, which when I was a young man, and my mother and father died, for seven years became my mother and father. I could not have asked for better.

Teachers who took me to the side, and told me if you can make 100, on this test you can make 100, on all.

Those who without sparing my feelings told me I was wrong.

Those who held my hand for a precious time, and let me go.

The merry spirits in my head that beat a joyful cadence.

Lynne Carrier, without whose edits I could not survive.

Hilary Lawson Crane, who helped me with a difficult poem.

Linda Opie, who, graciously allowed me publish my poem about her eyes.

My fourth grade phonics teacher from Alabama, who helped me learn how to read, and warned me-- I would talk like her. She gave me the gift of a southern-hillbilly voice, inside my head and out, turning words and thoughts into music.

Lynne Carrier, for giving me my strong, inspirational daughters Sarah, and Nicole.

Susan Clemens, for giving me my strong, inpirational daughter Dorothy.

William Reeves, my high school coach who didn't fill my head with impossible sports dreams.

Thomas Jefferson School of Law whose teachers allowed me accomplish my dreams.

The Federal and State Courts in San Diego, California, and the high principled, good-hearted legal community that works therein, which for over 30 years has shaped and honed my mind to make me a better person than I would have been.

Acknowledgments

I thank you evil, and you too sadness for each day putting your best game on the table for me to play against, and reminding me life is worth the fight.

Thanks to the little girl in the fourth grade who kicked my ass in the art contest at George C. Weimer Elementary School. I still think my poster to get black top on the playground was best. But, the Principal, Mr. Arnett said the judges of the art contest, because I drew "Mickey Mouse" in my poster, thought my picture was not original. I got more out of that Second Place finish than if I'd won; I received a compass for the future.

Introduction

I had a dream I was out to dinner with Emily, John, and Willie. They were interested in our modern life and asked if men and women still broke each other's hearts? "Yeah," I told them, "You guys could still make a good living on earth." Then I stopped and said, "You are, maybe better than in the day. Emily, you too." They looked at me as if they understood their importance and Willie said, "Well, we were the greatest poets on earth and for some strange reason we are here in your dream! What the hell have you written?"

I replied, "I've written some poems over the years and maybe you'd like to read them." Ignoring me, Emily said, "So we still don't know where we came from." Keats replied, "Yeah, you would think if we could go to the moon we would know more about ourselves. You guys are still on the shore of the world, thinking until nothingness sinks." Then Willie looked at me and said, "So this is the dream in death that comes and in that dream you want us to read your poetry." John laughed, and said, "Wake this guy up so we can get out of here!" I told them not to get upset. I didn't intend them to be in my dream. Exasperated Emily said, "This is a wild night in a dream. We don't have a compass or map to chart our way out."

I grabbed John's arm and told him I flunked out of San Diego State University because of him. I got an "F" in ballroom dancing. It was 1962, I was a college freshman playing football without a scholarship and washing dishes in the cafeteria. Time I should have been studying for classes I spent reading poems in the library and trying to write an essay about the urn.

You see, the final examination in my ballroom dancing class was graded on how well you danced with a girl. Dancing with girls was the reason I took the class; but, you would be graded dancing with your partner, and I didn't want a girl to get a bad grade; so I didn't show for the final. I asked Emily and Willie to consider I got the "F" because of one of their favorite virtues, chivalry. They looked at me as if to ask, "Dancing is a college course?" "But I did it for love," I told them. "I was proud of my "F" in ballroom dancing; and the reason I flunked out was I spent all my time studying your poetry. Do you know how many Cs you have to make to bring up ½ unit of F to a C?

During my divorces my ex-wives didn't object to getting the houses and me getting my poems. At the time I thought it was a steal. The three poets looked at me like I was a fool. "But, I did it for my poetry," I told them. They laughed.

I explained I'd written poems all my life, kept them under beds, in suitcases, lugged them to wherever I lived and worked. Kept them in school and police department lockers; in law office filing cabinets, even pulled them to safety out of the trunks of wrecked and impounded cars. My poems have been the most steady thing in my life, sometimes the only thing.

Willie said, "Screw your poems! We want back to life and out of your goddamned dream." John pushed me and yelled, "Wake up!" Then Emily screamed, "No, don't wake him! If you wake him, what will happen to us? If he wakes, we might cease to exist anymore; we might go back from where we came."

Table of Contents

Acknowledgments v

Introduction vii

When the carnival returns 1

Talking to Elves 5

Double-Barreled Lucy 9

Bigfoot 13

Stirring the stars 15

The words she said 17

Herod's Night 19

The River Ouse (Virginia Woolf) 21

The not my pants defense 23

Patti Smith 25

French fries & ketchup 29

Oh my Gosh Santa Claus 31

The traffic light 33

Hey Freud, holster your cigar 35

My jump from heaven 37

Manhattan 41

Hunting the what-about 43

Understanding Miranda 45

The Garbage Man 49

Attorney Let'emgo 53

Pete Wilson 57

kettle of stars 59

Opus on God and Monkey 63

Ode to abandoned police station 69

Table of Contents

The Ghost of Judy Mae Hess............................73

the firefly ring 75

Old Joe's dirt..77

Jewish Girls and the Devil's Fiddle Strings......79

Linda Opie's Eyes...81

What is the weather?......................................85

Dinner at the Ritz 87

Target Practice for the Gods 91

Love Songs Past 99

The Measured Man 101

A guy out for a look...................................... 103

Looking for flying reindeer............................ 105

Kathy again 107

The ghost in my pencil point 109

Columbus.. 111

Nails & Wings.. 113

The Other Fisherman 115

My true love... 119

My Explosive Heart....................................... 121

The double alibi defense 123

The Shepherd's Eye 127

Elegy to Hank 129

The Studebaker... 135

superpower of enough................................... 139

The Sorcerer Celeste 141

ghosts in me... 143

The place on the door.................................... 145

I survive without you..................................... 147

The girl with shotgun eyes 149

Master of my Pants....................................... 151

The Author 153

When the carnival returns

At the entrance to the carnival,
a sign read "Your fortune for a Penny."
The old lady had a closed smile
and fingered up my money;
then she peered into her crystal ball,
and asked my girlfriend Calli
if her father's name was Zeus?
"You're out with a deity!" she told me;
then smiled with a missing tooth.
"Better hold her tight!
The carnival can steal a girl's heart.
The Ferris Wheel throws love,
beyond the clouds into the universe.
It swings hearts toward the stars
way out beyond Earth and Venus,
farther than the planet Mars.
Somewhere up in the high airs,
that's where young hands pull apart.
The Carnival plays below the clouds
then moves on to other towns."
I complained, "That was not a fortune."
The old lady grabbed my hands,
looked at my palms, and said, "It's true!
You will perform your lovesick rhymes
in an empty auditorium like a fool.

No love will sit in the balconies
holding her breath for you."
The old woman closed her stand
then backed away as Calli held my hand.
We ended up sitting in the grandstand
among customers who cheered,
then stood to twist their necks
to see jugglers, clowns, and men on stilts,
while barkers yelled, "Peanuts! Peanuts!"
From within the crowd,
the Ringmaster picked me out,
to be part of his act.
I sauntered down to the center of the tent;
where he gave me his whip and hat
and introduced me as the main act.
Then he ran, for he was a clown disguised.
A performer was being carried out
on a gurney flat upon his back.
An elephant had deigned to tiptoe
on the high wire rope that now hung loose
on both sides of the track.
It was my big chance.
So, I told the crowd my stories,
and gave my song and dance.
I saw Calli laughing in the stands.
The clown had taken my empty seat
and he was holding both her hands.
With my songs and jokes I danced.
My rhymes I'd toss like silk scarves
to drift like magic doves across the crowd.
My phrases were death defying leaps
as they flew high in the big tent;
then would plunge toward my feet,

only, to be in mid-air caught before they hit.
The crowd heard my rhymes and jokes
and warmed me when it laughed.
Calli got lost in their applause,
and I looked all night with a broken heart.
That night the carnival packed its tents.
Went on to its next performance.
The fortune teller with the missing tooth
wrapped the excitement up in canvas;
tied the tent poles with dirty ropes;
put the cotton candy in a truck
and drove away without a look.
I heard Calli left with the carnival
and sideshow hustlers on the bus;
that she dumped the clown and traveled
to wherever the carnival shacked up.
She had some children, one by a fire eater,
and the last everyone heard
she had left her kids with her mother
and was studying acting in Hollywood.
I could have chased after Calli;
shacked up in countless towns,
fallen asleep to the calliope
outside my window with its haunting sounds.
Instead I've polished my performance
before an audience of ghosts.
Sometimes off in the distance
I hear a calliope's notes.
The chords echo in my heart beats
when I think it's coming close.
One day when the carnival returns
with an audience in the big tent,
I will no longer entertain my ghosts.

Under the tent surrounded by the crowds
I'll fearless tell my rhymes and jokes;
compete for laughter with the clowns;
Toss my thoughts into the big tent;
where they'll entertain the crowds.
Should they fall crumpled on the ground;
I'll dodge the hooves of horses,
and release some colored balloons;
feed the lumbering elephants peanuts;
pick up from the ground my broken words,
and through the legs of the man on stilts
look to see if Calli's in the crowd.

---

* The idea came from a traveling carnival in West Virginia, south of Dupont High School, in the City of Belle, 1958. It would be years later when I finished the rhyme—almost an old man; well, an old man. The idea had hung around in my head for a long time; and I jotted down some notes decades before I finished.

The idea of losing your love at a carnival was born by the great Kanawha River, with smells of pink cotton candy, a single ferris wheel, a Calliope's notes drifting up into a starry night and a pretty Jewish girl named Joan. I was in the 8th grade. Of course by the time I finished the poem, years later, decades later, I'd been to lots of carnivals. But, the first one, you never forget.

I've only been back to West Virginia once. I visited the little towns I grew up in, 2 & 3 Qt. Mi. Creek, St. Albans, and Belle. Just drove around, got out of my rental car and walked around. It was long before I finished the poem. I was in West Virginia on a product liability case to conduct a deposition. In my late thirties, a Californian coming back home to where he grew up. The thing I remember most is everyone talked like me. I have a hillbilly southern accent, and I had come home to where I would have been had I stayed. All these people were talking like me; and, it felt very warm. I had been gone for so long and now I was surrounded by voices that spoke like me; although, I didn't know a soul and my onetime presence as a boy had been forgotten; almost everyone had moved.

One day you look back, even though you are surrounded in happiness, and come to realize the breadth of emptiness of what could have been in your life. It plays like an entertainer in a theater who walks around on an empty stage, looks out into vacant seats, and in that cerebral world for a moment remembers what her hair smelled like. Maybe he tells a joke to the empty seats, dances a little jig, then gets out quick before he suffocates.

Talking to Elves

Remember that night,
we awoke to a dog's bark,
rolled over and kissed
and for a moment thought
about what the dog barks meant.
You told me you dreamed
you'd been talking to elves,
but became unsettled
with yourself because
you forgot what they'd said.
I thought it was absurd
to dream of elves.
Tears formed in your eyes
when I told you I didn't believe
elves existed in your dreams.
But, you became amused
when I suggested you'd been confused
by dog barks that you'd heard;
and you'd mistaken dog barks
for the words of Elves.
Oh, you laughed it off,
that you could have mistaken barks
for the words of Elves.
We decided you'd write them down
and we'd read them in the morn'.

But, the next day
you were dismayed
when you tried to read your words;
it seems the words of Elves
could only be understood in dreams.
The only time Elves make sense
is when you're a-snooze.
Remember when,
in the wee hours of morn'
after Elves and dogs were gone;
we held hands,
and at the tops of our lungs
howled at the moon, . . .
'til someone turned the lights on.
We were surprised at ourselves
for acting insane,
and wondered if Elves
were somehow to blame.
After that night,
I heard you talk in your sleep,
watched you sit up;
then, jump out of bed
looking for a pen to write down
the words Elves said.
Worry not your pretty head
your Elf words I have saved.
You forgot the Elf words boxed
beneath our bed kept safe.
You must have thought
the words could never have been read
'cause you left them all abandoned
in that box beneath our bed.
Since you left,

there are some nights
I fall out of sleep
to a dog bark that keeps me awake,
falling in and out of a conscious state;
still remembering what I dreamt;
then turn over to think to myself
about barking dogs,
and whether you still talk to Elves.

     No, I made this poem up. I have never known anyone that spoke to Elves in their dreams, or in real life. Sometimes, a fellow writes about something for the hell of it. It would have been more interesting if the gal had run off with the Elf.

CHARLES N. GUTHRIE

Double-Barreled Lucy

Oh, Lucy, Lucy, Lucy,
When she struts her stuff,
she's a double-barreled shotgun, . . .
            ready to go off!

Since Lucy left me, . . .
my life is not much fun.
Lucy, Lucy, Lucy
            She's a double-barreled gun!

Sweet double-barreled Lucy.
Sweet, sweet Lucy, you're the gun!
Without double-barreled Lucy, . . .
            life is not, not, not, much fun.

Lucy, Lucy, Lucy, . . .
bring back your big, big gun.
Since you left my life, . . .
            I ain't had any fun.

Lucy, Lucy, Lucy, . . .
I hope you've kept your barrels warm!
My sweet double-barreled Lucy, . . .
            I'm so alone without your gun.

Without your lov'n arms
I'm done! Done! Done! Done! Done!
Oh my Lucy, Lucy, Lucy, . . .
       Bring back your big, big, gun.

Blow me to high heavens
or send me straight to hell
hold me in the arms, . . .
       of your great big shotgun barrel.

Hug me with both barrels
so tight you make me squeal.
Squeeze me 'til the trigger pulls, . . .
       and blow me straight to hell.

Oh Lucy, Lucy, Lucy,
After I've been blown to hell.
All of heaven's Angels
       will ring their jealous bells.

The Angels will be pissed off an earth girl
could make me feel like the gods;
They'll throw away their halos, . . .
       and stop playing with their harps.

Double-Barreled Lucy

Oh Lucy, Lucy, Lucy,
You'll make the Devil angry too, . . .
That he can't tempt a soul to hell, . . .
        half as well as you.

Oh Lucy, Lucy, Lucy,
Come on back to me
We can dodge the harps and halos, . . .
        dangerous though they be.

Oh, Lucy, Lucy, Lucy, . . .
You're back with me at last
this is such a great day, . . .
        of course it'll be a blast!

Oh, my sweet, sweet Lucy,
my Lu-Lu, . . . Ceeee, Ceeee, Ceeee!
That big shotgun that you strut, . . .
        I want it to swallow me.

Load me in your stomach
and aim me at the stars.
Then with all your fireworks, . . .
        blow me past the moon to Mars.

Oh, Lucy, Lucy, Lucy,
When you strut your stuff,
you're a double-barreled shotgun, . . .
       ready to go off.

Oh Lucy, Lucy, Lucy,
I think I'll write another verse
Even though it's dangerous, . . .
       my love for you's perverse!

Oh Lucy, Lucy, Lucy,
When you strut your stuff,
you're a double-barreled shotgun, . . .
       ready to go off.

Written in 1963, on the back of an envelope in the parking lot by the old Aztec football field, at San Diego State.

Bigfoot

2 years, 3 days, and away it goes,
I had a girlfriend with large feet and toes.
Not embarrassingly big like a kangaroo's;
but, in truth, I could easily wear her shoes.
For the record I wore her tennis shoes;
not high heels she wore with hose,
or shoes she wore with girly clothes.
Her big feet were my special delight;
but, she could not accept her feet
were an attractive part of my life.
To myself I named her Bigfoot
and kept her nickname under lock.
The day we parted I didn't hold back.
I begged "Bigfoot" please don't leave,
"I love you and your big feet."
"That's what I thought,"
She said with a grimace,
Then tossed her shoes into my closet.
All that was left of Bigfoot were her shoes.
They've been in my closet since she left.
Sometimes I wear them for days of twos.
Oh, I've tried to cut her memory loose
by tossing her shoes into the trash;
but, I pull them back with a laugh.
More than one friend has asked,

holding their finger over their nose,
"Why do you keep these old tennis shoes?"
No one has ever suspected
the shoes of an old lover I've collected.
I suppose Bigfoot and I are through;
but, as hard as I've tried,
I can't throw away her shoes.

Stirring the stars

The red light grabbed her by the waist
and held her at the corner wait.
She gave a pause, . . .
then with her eyes
gave me a spiteful glance
burning through my prowl car's glass.
My imagination was on fire.
My patrol car was aflame.
The red light loosed about her waist,
and the green light beckoned her away.
She walked into the moving night
leaving me and my desire
a-smolder in a patrol car.

Off the Island of Nantucket, . . .
sailing on white sheets I hunt.
No laws except the Captain's
and nature's rules to keep.
From beneath the sea she surges.
Eyes flashing orange and turquoise fire!
Each eye full of vengeance and desire.

The harpoon thrown and taunt the line.
Together in one ball we twine
until the whale's foam blows white.
Then we're washed up on bed sheets
in a forgotten land.
A garden gate opens at our push.
We munch on strawberries and plums.
Her face a bowl of midnight's
coal black soup,
and a million twinkling stars
for me to taste.
I dip my spoon into the night,
and stir the stars until the dark
is filled with light,
and light is filled with dark.
Take my time, kiss, and sip her lips,
swallow the stars one by one,
until we ask, "What it was
that painted each and orphaned
us on the streets?"

The words she said

Once there was a girl who wrote poetry.
At the time I didn't appreciate her melody.
Once there was a girl that took hand and pen
and wrote words so pure and clean
they could cut down trees with honesty.
But her words could not cut me.
No, her words could not cut me.
Like a statue of rock and dry bone I was dead
immune to all the words she said.

Once there was a girl who wrote poetry.
But, now in a different world I breathe.
It is now in this world so remote,
I understand the words she wrote,
and they break my heart, they break my heart.
Upon my knees I fall and cry out,
"Why can't I go back to when I was dead,
to wake up understanding the words she said?"

Herod's Night

Oh Herod's Night, Oh Herod's Night,
    the bureaucrats stole baby Christ.
Oh Herod's night, Oh Herod's Night
    No Eastern Star or kings in sight.
Hark, hark ,the city's honking horns
    Christ was taken by entrepreneurs.
Christmas 'tis forever gone
    'Tis Winter Holidays from now on.
No Star of Bethlehem atop the trees
    just bland bulbs and ornaments.
Christmas symbols have been taxed
    and moved aside by bureaucrats;
They've been replaced by scales of justice,
    sugar gavels and black gowns.
Oh Herod's Night, Oh Herod's Night,
    the bureaucrats stole baby Christ.
Oh Herod's night, Oh Herod's Night
    no Eastern Star or Kings in sight.
No manger in Central Park,
    no Christian symbols in the square;
The Teethie smiles of Bureaucrats
    are about the city everywhere.
Old St. Nicholas takes his place;
    his meaning lost in melting snow.

Since becoming the front man for the state
    he acts like he does not know
how he got his job in the first place.
    Oh! Oh! The gleeful Ho, Ho, Ho's!
Christmas has been stolen, there it goes.
    Behold a modern crucifixion
where Christ is pushed into the margin.
    Soldiers no longer carry swords and spears,
just political correctness, glue and scissors.
    Oh! Herod's Night. Oh! Herod's Night.

    No Holy Star, or kings in sight.
No Christian symbols in the square.
    Teethie bureaucrats everywhere.
The meaning of Christmas is all gone
    'Tis Winter Holidays from now on.
Yet, Santa Claus can come and go
    his meaning lost in melting snow.

The River Ouse (Virginia Woolf)

What said the voices
      in sounds coming from the dead?
A tribe of talking, coughing demons, . . .
      were pounding in her head.
They joined her private conversations,
      they talked, listened and replied;
they brought up ugly topics
      to her perfect mind.
They were aware of goings on outside
      the windows of her eyes.
They were the babble of an audience
      that awaits the curtain's rise;
They were the water talking, talking, talking
      for her to jump inside.
They were croaking frogs in unison,
      calling out Virginia's name.
The cane, and hat, the letters, and the stone
      were all clues about the demons
inside her head going wrong.
      Percolating from the waters
the voices jumped inside her mind.
      A pirate ship of lunatics
laid claim upon her deck;

partied on her bridge;
      confused her compass off its course;
smeared insanity on her windows;
      then looked out through her eyes;
to watch the waters
      of the River Ouse slowly rise.

The not my pants defense

The prosecution's opening statement wasn't long.
"The officer stuck a finger into Mickey's pocket
and five rocks of cocaine jumped out and sang a song.
The rocks in Mickey's pocket made Mickey a crook."

The defense attorney was brief, but made his point.
"Mickey put someone else's pants on by mistake.
Why Mickey was as surprised as those shocked cops
when out of his pocket jumped five singing rocks."

The Officer testified, "The singing rocks of cocaine
were in harmony as if they'd been singing all day."
But, since the pants fit Mickey, he hadn't asked,
"Whose pants they were and who wore them last?"

Mickey told the jury, "In the first place,
because the pants fit he'd made the mistake."
But he didn't say whose pants he'd worn,
or where he'd been when he put them on.

Then into the courtroom walked Mrs. Brown
owner of the house from which Mickey ran.
She said, "Those pants don't belong to Mickey.
They belong to my husband who came home early."

Mickey got scared and dressed in a hurry.
He grabbed my husband's pants in a flurry;
jumped out the window and over the sill;
last I saw he was headed for the hill."

Mrs. Brown's husband was called for rebuttal.
He told the jury he knew he was in trouble;
"But those pants with the rocks are not mine.
Mickey and my wife are out to get my behind!"

The defense argued the rocks were in slumber
until rudely awakened by the officer's finger.
The prosecutor said, "They were ready to croon,
wide awake in the pocket and humming a tune."

The jury listened to the rocks sing their song
then retired to decide if Mickey had done wrong.
The jury foreman chuckled after Mickey's conviction,
"Nobody believed the story of a hurried fornication."

The prosecutor smiled and made the suggestion,
"Next time Mickey should get an innocent excuse,
one that would make him look like a gentleman.
Maybe then his next jury would cut him loose."

The judge didn't like rocks singing in her court;
so, she sentenced Mickey one year per rock;
but, from the bench she gave Mickey some advice.
"Next time you hear rocks singing in your pocket,
take your pants off, and run for your life!"

Patti Smith

The spinning Cola bottle stopped
in a circle of classmates.
The bottle's lips pointed
at her surprised face.
She was on her knees
and the spinner made a joke,
then refused to give a kiss
and her heart broke.
Again the bottle spun,
her disappointment hidden;
inside crying she ran home;
passed her mother in the kitchen.
Then alone in her bedroom
she sobbed her way to sleep.
And while she slept a witch
kissed her on the cheek;
and conjured up an incantation
and on her image put a hex
that every eye on her reflection
would see a perfect face.
When I saw her picture in a magazine
wearing that straw hat I shut my eyes
and turned away pretending she wasn't seen.
After all, I knew I'd never be
closer than a picture on a page.

Oh, I tried very hard to forget her face.
But, upon my wall her picture hung,
that wall inside my head.
Oh, you know the one, the one
with a thousand pretty faces a guy remembers
but about which nothing's said.
The incantation didn't happen over night.
The next morning she still thought
her face was an ugly fright.
There was a long and coming wait
for a guy named Mapplethorpe
to give her the big break.
Then with a camera's click,
her face moved across the nation
over night it splashed
and she became a sensation.
But, good looks can be a prison
from which there is no escape;
and once again she cried
not because she wanted love--
now she wanted to be understood!
She mocked her perfect face,
posing crazed, embracing radical politics,
and wrote love songs that amazed.
But she couldn't break the witch's hex
that made her image perfect.
When she became old her face
turned from flower petal grace
to one of monstrous elegance;
and still the world was amazed.
Oh, I'm not the only guy who didn't realize
the girl in the hat would haunt his life.
On that wall inside my head

she would hang around forever perfect
as the witch had said.
I've not the guts to tell fantasies I've dreamt; but,
countless men have put her picture by their beds;
untold is the joy she's launched inside their heads.
There will always be the question
debated by fans and detractors in our nation;
whether she's a real person, a goddess or a demon;
or a little girl from Pennsylvania's German Town
that got her picture taken.

    Patti Smith, what a pretty girl. I fell in love with her when I saw her wearing a straw hat in her most famous photograph. Heard her interviewed on the Mike Douglas TV show, and realized she has a southern, hillbilly accent like myself. I've never met her.

    You know when you write a poem about a famous person; and, I've written several in this book; you write about the high points, and the high points are there for you to grab in the history books and magazines. Its harder, for me, to write a poem about someone I know. You just know too much.

French fries & ketchup

I was a bad boy,
        don't you, . . .
                don't you see?
I was too proud,
        too proud to buy—
                to buy her French fries & ketchup
        when he could buy her steak;
So I took my famous, . . .
        Oh so famous walk,
                and threw it in her face.
I was a bad boy,
        don't you, . . .
                don't you see?
I was too proud,
        to proud to be good,
                but now I know, . . .
        that she would have stayed,
you see she would have stayed
        because she told me she liked
                French fries and ketchup
                        just as well as steak.

But, I was a bad boy,
      don't you, . . .
            don't you see?
I was too proud of my fate
      to share French fries and ketchup
            when he could buy her steak.
But now I know too late
      she would have stayed, . . .
            she would have stayed with me.
Now I've got some money
      that I didn't have that day
            when I swapped love
for my pride, . . .
      and let her get away.
I was a bad boy, . . .
      don't you, don't you see?
            I was too proud to understand
she chose French fries and ketchup
      because she wanted to be with me.

Oh my Gosh Santa Claus

Oh my gosh Santa Claus
I've got to tell you a story.
It's about Ms. Betty, age 33,
who sat beneath her Christmas tree;
She looked sexy
after being good all year;
but now she felt so naughty
with a Christmas affair
with a man 34.

Oh my gosh Santa Claus
I've got to tell you a story.
It's about Mr. Charlie, age of 34,
who sat beneath a Christmas tree.
He looked handsome
after living like a Spartan
almost to year's end;
feeling guilty he was happy
having an affair with a woman 33.

Oh my gosh Santa Claus
can you be over 33, and still believe;
believe in flying reindeer with a sleigh;
or is it too late to sit on Santa's knee
and ask what gift you'll receive?
Too late for selfish thoughts;
or romantic whims?
Mr. Claus, could you give Betty and Charlie
a gift that might be difficult for your Elves?
A roaring ball of love to juggle between themselves;
Santa Claus please accept my assurances
Betty and Charlie are wise enough to play with fires,
smart enough to juggle their loves around the rocks.
Oh, my gosh, Santa Claus, it's really getting hot.

The traffic light

The lonely traffic light
rules the intersection
with colors bright.
Each color taking turn
staining the empty streets
and water puddles
with red-scarlets
limes and yellows.
Behind a billboard
in the squad car parked
the patrolman looks intent
at the intersection's mouth
for an errant motorist
passing through,
who might break a color's rule
by not coming to a stop
for the meaning of scarlet.
He watches the traffic light's
"... Stops ..." and "... Goes ..."
But on the street nothing moves
for which his eyes were designed;
as the colors yellow, red and lime
on ghost travelers do not shine.
But for the beat
of the patrolman's heart

the world is quiet.
There is nothing left,
but to sit, and think about
his life's wait,
and what lays silent.
He wonders why by fate
out of all the stars that blink
in all the universe he is trapped
and on this planet placed
to hunt and eat; and yet,
allowed to travel in his thought
as far as imagination can take;
yet, is still in his body trapped.
The traffic light can only blink.
It wonders not from where it came.
Nor does it care for thoughts of travelers,
with its colors scarlet, yellow, lime,
or understand the meanings that its colors bear.
For the patrolman's steady heart beats
there is nothing in the dark that pines.
Nothing moves toward where he sits
or jumps out of the dark with applause;
to render recognition to his mind;
or offers support as would a friendly god.
The patrolman cannot prevent his thought.
He does not know what his thoughts mean
to things of which to him remain unseen;
nor how thoughts are understood
by things going and coming in another world.

Hey Freud, holster your cigar

Hey Freud, holster your cigar.
I've got the answer you were looking for.
The question that stumped you,
"What do women want?"
Take a listen to my thought.
You underestimated femininity
with your theory about envy.
I've come up with "the big envy theory"
where gals want the whole male body.
Observe women at a party;
how their husbands make them happy.
Watch the men perform their tricks.
"Honey, can you get us drinks?
Don't forget the dip and chips.
Now run and play with the other men
and let us girls talk in the kitchen."
What women want and it's really not much,
is to talk about their men over lunch.
Sigmund, here is my hunch.
A man does not have to be handsome or rich
as a man wearing pants is enough.
All women want and it's really not much
is to be able to talk to each other about us.
Sigmund, your envy theory is partially true;
it just doesn't account for womenkind's ego.

For that reason you missed the mark
as to what women really, really want!
Let me humbly present my big envy theory.
What women want most
is to be able to talk with other gals about
any excuse of a man they've got.
To casually with the other girls confide
in the kitchen with a smile, "I've got one too!"
But, just so I don't shock the world
like you, Mr. Sigmund Freud;
just so my big theory of what women want,
doesn't by the reader get misconstrued--
as women not having what men have got.
What women mean by, "I've got one too,"
is to say, "I've got a man just like you!"

My jump from heaven

The audience on earth was magnanimous.
    I felt the kisses and Hip, Hip, Hurrahs!
Heard their gathered friendly voices,
    and hands slapping with applause.

Why, I tell you I could take a stride
    into and out the crowd's mouth.
Could sit upon a tooth and soliloquize
    I was so complacent with myself.

But, on that tooth I tempted fate.
    I dared the curtain shut its mouth.
My rhymes became too confident
    until I could not quench the crowd.

I lay broken in the limelight.
    Words forgotten to my song.
My dreams of entertainment
    lost and gone so very wrong.

A bird from the heavens
    grabbed me wiggling in its arms
and with me screaming in its talons
    flew me to the stars.

By the time we entered the afterlife
    I had told the bird a joke.
My hope was to make the planets laugh
    and gods of heaven not provoke.

Riding into heaven on its shoulders
    singing rhymes and humming bars,
I heard the gods were having auditions
    for new arrivals to be stars.

I stood in heaven's call-back line,
    with a thousand other poets;
I was there to entertain
    with my rhymes and verses.

Behind heaven's curtain on the stage
    with my words and rhymes as props
I heard the talk of cabbage and my name.
    So, I decided to tell some jokes.

When heaven's curtain rose,
    I saw good and evil's gathered hearts.
Devils gave me Hip, Hip, Hurrahs,
    Angels blew me kisses from their mouths.

Why, I had them laughing in the aisles.
    As if they were on earth,
remembering life's joys and loves
    they even laughed at death.

My jump from heaven

Then heaven's thunder clapped.
    They threw cabbage and tomatoes.
Angels drank wine and devil's smoked.
    The gods didn't like my jokes.

You see the gods became angry
    because I'd broken heaven's rule.
No jokes about eternity's absurdity
    because it made god look like a fool.

I had made angels and devils laugh
    at the promise of eternal life
pointing out if life can't cease
    there is no excitement left.

I didn't know jokes about god's reward
    were in heaven not allowed.
I was pulled off the stage with a thud
    and trampled by the crowd.

I'd never given it a thought
    to stay in heaven one might not.
The thing I disliked in heaven most
    were stars and planets underfoot.

There was a place on Old Harp Bridge,
    where angels went to jump;
Where someone wrote on the ledge,
    "Leave heaven when you want."

Looking down before I leapt,
    moving closer to the edge;
I saw stars and comets under foot,
    earth in a starry nest.

Landing outside a church,
    in a storm of wedding rice,
I asked a guest was I on earth,
    and for some advice.

Revelers laughed at my garbled sounds
    as half my words were left in heaven;
They didn't ask me to recite my rhymes
    because I had a ghostly conversation.

I promised revelers for a bite of cake
    and a sip of their champagne
I would tell them of my jump from heaven
    which made me look insane.

Again on earth behind the curtain
    with stars up in the sky.
I had a second chance to entertain
    and could joke that I could die.

Manhattan

As fast as you can, cab driver,
as fast as you can go,
drive me to Manhattan;
don't stop by the road.
Demons are outside your windows.
Right now they are smiling at me.
Here, cab driver, take my fifty
and, Drive me! Drive me! Drive me!
In Manhattan there are no demons
because Manhattan never sleeps.
It's a city of light without shadows
that makes the demons retreat.
My heart is surrounded by demons.
They swim in my blue, blue blood.
My heart is surrounded by demons.
They fit so snug, snug, snug.
They kiss my lips like a snake.
They suck the breath I take.
Hot darts are the eyes of demons.
They pierce through the window glass.
Their little fists knock on my temples.
They have camping gear and sharp instruments.
Blood red matches spill from their pockets.
They're building fires and heating up spears.
Forget the red lights and yellows;

get me over the East River.
I want to be in Manhattan forever.
Don't want demons inside my soul.
Don't want them to set up camp in my temple
where they will curse 'til I'm old.
Oh gosh! Look at the East River.
It's dark, on the run and it's cold.
Guess what Cab Driver;
we must be in Manhattan;
because the demons are gone, gone, gone!
Some of them got in my temple.
Out of kindness I didn't let them escape.
I kept them locked up in my body
just so you'd be safe.
But, now that they're gone it's such a relief.
I know you must think I'm crazy.
You can park now and get your fifty;
now that you got me here safely.

Hunting the what-about

It was as bad as it goes.
I had lost control of my own prose.
I had lost the knack of what to write.
Each day with pencil, clock and note
I'd set out to hunt the what-about,
that elusive prey so hard to recognize,
you know each has its own disguise.
Behind a cup of coffee and some books
I'd camouflage myself like I had roots.
There I'd wait to jump out and surprise
a what-about for me to write.
But, I couldn't find a what-about.
I'd go home at night and think
I'll never catch a what-about.
I finally gave up the hunt.
But then guess what?
Suddenly, I could write.
I could write about anything I want!
Write about anything I thought;
From the horns of a goat to a piano note,
and I've got to tell you I'm about to gloat
about the what-about I wrote.

Deciding what to write about is what hunting the what-about is about. Sometimes, you want to write but there is nothing to write about. They call it writer's block. So, for lack of anything to write about, I wrote about hunting a subject, a "what-about," to write about.

Understanding Miranda

Miranda was a gangster
who made her money on the street.
She had a code of honor
she held with some conceit.
One day a line of devil's tooth
surprised her like a snake;
and before she could push it off
it bit her on the face.
That's when she started selling tooth
not for the gangster's plate;
but, because it was for herself
'cause now she had to use it.
When her gangster buddies
heard she was bitten by the snake
she was no longer asked
to look for cops and drive the cars
in burglaries and robberies
then party after at the bars.
It wasn't long before she cracked
and was seen crying in the street;
asking passers that she'd meet,
How many times can you kiss the devil
before you're kissed back on the cheek?
She didn't get many answers.
People looked at her with awe.

Then she'd scream at them,
"Well, the answer's on the wall!"
Then one dark and rainy night,
broken down and lost,
she sold some of her devil's tooth
to an undercover narc.
With her hands cuffed tight,
sitting in a van, . . .
she started telling lies
about her sale to the man.
She heard, You've got the right to silence;
to be questioned with an attorney;
and everything you tell us
will be used to make you guilty.
Then the cop took a pause,
the pause cops always take,
looked her in the eyes and asked,
Do you understand your rights?
The gangsters feared her words would spill
a story that would lock them all up tight.
The junkies thought she'd sit in jail
until the devil scared up her bail.
Or, she could have made a contract
with the chief devil of the state;
who turns one crook against the next
so the first can get a break.
You see, the court will sell absolution
for the promise not use drugs again;
and, in court a crooked finger's point
from a drug seller's ex-best friend.
Did she avoid a prosecution?
No one knows if she told a tale;
casting blame on someone else,

to get a lesser bail.
Maybe she made the old cop smile;
and caused him to give that dime.
You know the one to call your Mom,
or for a taxi ride.
Miranda was a Princess,
the Princess of the Street.
The crooks knew she would be silent
and she would never squeak.
The junkies think the devil
who walks the street is real.
He scared up money for her bail
and Miranda kissed the devil
when released from county jail.
She's not been seen for weeks.
Crooks are too scared
to ask the cops if she snitched.
No one knows her whereabouts,
not the gangsters or the freaks.
But, she's back in business selling tooth
says the word-of-mouth on the streets;
from the window of her mother's house
cause she's got to make attorney fees.
Or she could be in that program,
the one for her protection;
living in a safe house like a pigeon
who gave evidence to the prosecution.
Friends have tried to reach her on the phone
but a voice says, "Leave Miranda alone!"
What's really known is she's been gone,
and her gangster buddies are on the run.
The answer to her question
that she asked out in the street,

How many times can you kiss the devil,
before you're kissed back on the cheek?
The answer is spray canned on the wall
of every slum town street.
The devil doesn't kiss a girl.
He bites her with his teeth.

The Garbage Man

The garbage man came early
in the morning to collect.
So, I left a note and money
so he would not suspect.

Placed it in an envelope
and taped it on the lid;
thanked him for his service
and all the work he did.

I heard the garbage truck
coming down the road.
The cans went bang and clank
as he would stop and go.

Not wanting to be witness
to a suicide by cans;
I was hiding in my house
peeking through the blinds.

The garbage man read my note,
then tossed it in the trash.
I waited for the crescendo
of my garbage cans to clash.

About ended relationships
the garbage man cared less;
photos torn up by my hands
he would carry off as trash.

He stomped upon the gas.
I heard the garbage spin.
A flock of circling birds
descended on my cans.

None ran with safety ropes
to save love letters from the dump.
No voice came from my house,
"Hey, garbage man, stop!"

The can's eyes were open.
The garbage man was gone.
His absence was my delusion
for he always hung around.

The garbage man one day
would come with noisy truck.
Stand in my steps behind me,
then break my front door lock.

Burgle me of last regret;
whether I left a note or money.
Look deep into my heart,
then carry off my body.

      In 1967, I lived in Pacific Beach, a community in the City of San Diego. 24 years old, working the night shift on the police department and sleeping in the day. Twice a week the garbage truck would drive by noisily picking up cans and putting trash on its back. The noise always woke me up. Sometimes a cop gets a call about the report of a death. Most were about natural causes. Sometimes we'd respond to suicides, car wreck fatalities, and some homicides. In those days, I drove an ambulance. Those experiences helped produce this poem. One day, long after police work, between court appearances as an attorney, I wrote the garbage man (most of it) and threw the notes into one of my poetry boxes. The notes lay there for years; then, I fished it out of the box. I'd forgotten what I'd written; after all, it was about garbage.

CHARLES N. GUTHRIE

Attorney Let'emgo

Attorney Let'emgo let out a moan.
His client's tale began in Mexico.
He'd drunk a bottle of Old Bevo.
Then drove his car passed the Border Patrol.
With a trail of police cars in his wake
in the back streets of L.A. he eluded the parade--
driving all the way to the San Francisco Gate.
When he got to Frisco he fell out of his car,
staggered to a house and opened the door.
The Frisco cops found him sleeping on the floor.
Arrested him and put him in cuffs.
Let'emgo said, "Stop! I've heard enough!
I'll take your case and get you off.
What is and what's not a burglary
is evidence no one can see.
A prosecutor must prove
beyond a reasonable doubt
that as a suspect enters a house
the intent inside of the suspect's heart
is to commit theft or a felony farce."
In court, Let'emgo made the argument
his client's drunkenness made him innocent.
Then added, better drunk than a crook!
My client entered the wrong house.
To steal was not his intent;

nor was it to commit a felony farce.
He had drunk too much and wanted to sleep.
The only intent in my client's head
was to go home and straight to bed.
Then in front of the jury Let'emgo
pulled out a bottle of Old Bevo.
He took a swig as he would argue
and to the jury put on a show
as he argued he drank the booze.
By the time he was through,
he didn't know where he was, or what to do.
He couldn't see if the jury was there.
A Bailiff had to lead him to his chair.
The jury was out for a few minutes,
and came back, "not guilty," unanimous!
Let'emgo was interviewed by the news.
Sober with coffee, he expounded his views.
He hoped the judge didn't think he was rude
because he had taken some snorts as he argued.
The judge ruled he shouldn't have drunk
in his argument; and, such antics unpunished
set a bad precedent.
She found Let'emgo guilty of contempt
for drinking booze without the court's consent.
He was sentenced to three days in the clink.
Three days more than his client.
Then the judge smiled down from her seat,
and said, "It should have been more, . . . but,
I liked Let'emgo's argument."
Since that verdict,
an awkward reputation follows Let'emgo in court.
He's the best attorney in San Francisco,
when he's drunk.

A middle aged man wearing a suit and tie sitting on the lobby floor of one of San Francisco's business towers, searching for guts to walk without an appointment into a woman's office I'd not seen since we were young. As I sat there drinking a cup of coffee and eating a bagel I thought about a gentleman's promise I had made decades earlier. The promise was one I came to regret, and like a battered warrior, not so grand as Odysseus, or victorious, I had returned home to the idea of her, and moored my life to the tower lobby floor. Sat there thinking of the Penelope in my life, who I had last seen, it seemed a thousand years ago. For me the atmosphere inside my heart was electric, absolutely heart pounding.

There was no business for me that day in San Francisco, except to walk around and show up for my flight to San Diego. I was flying back and forth on a weekly basis; but this day I was trying to find the strength to visit a woman I knew when we were both young. My thought was she might be leaving for lunch and by accident run into me. I would not break my promise to the other young man, of course now an old man, and if that happened I'd get to see her again. It was a sneaky logic. It wouldn't be more than Hello, and how are you doing; but mustering my guts was impossible and that's probably because I was hoping for something more.

I ate my bagel, drank my coffee and while I sat there wrote *Let'emgo*. Jotted the gist of the poem on a wrinkled napkin. The whole time thinking a security guard was going to ask me to leave; but after all, it was San Francisco. Sitting on the floor of the lobby, wearing a suit and tie, eating a bagel probably looked conservative. After more than an hour I folded my napkin notes, placed *Let'emgo* into my wallet, took a deep breath, and walked out. Got on the Bart to Oakland and with Attorney *Let'emgo* snug in my wallet, made my Southwest flight back to San Diego. *Let'emgo* and I have been good friends ever since.

CHARLES N. GUTHRIE

Pete Wilson

People stop and gawk
at the iron man who doesn't speak;
standing by a sidewalk on a public street.
Up close they walk and look;
then on the pavement by his feet,
they stop to read his resume
that argues for higher placement
of a statue with his name.
Someplace better you would think,
than a public sidewalk,
for the Governor of the state;
who came within a sore throat,
most think, of being President.
His statue should be high above
the common people on the street.
Normal folks should not come close,
as to be near enough to speak; yet,
some stand so close they nod and wink
as if they talk with Pete.
Republicans say it was wrong
to leave Pete all alone.
Why, he should be in a parthenon
with other legends gone.
Democrats say it was wrong
to erect a statue of Iron Pete,

because after all; as yet,
he is not deceased.
He should be melted down
and only after he's buried and gone
should his statue be put up again;
and then, only when it's shown
a Republican can go to heaven.
The political pundits opine,
all the smilin' by Iron Pete,
as he stands there on the street
means he's still politickin'
for less government.
But, we all know the reason
that his critics are upset;
it's because his constant smilin'
is so very permanent.

My law office is in the Old Spreckels Building, at First & Broadway, at the end of Second Street, on the east side where Horton Plaza begins. I can look out the window to where there is a statue of Pete Wilson. It's the friendliest statue in Horton Plaza. There is a list of Pete's accomplishments imbedded in the sidewalk. My thought was I might write a strong and humorous poem about him. I hope I succeeded. I sent the poem out to newspapers, radio stations, TV stations, and local San Diego magazines and not one response. Maybe it's not as good as I think.

kettle of stars

In the restaurant of desires,
before the menu met her eyes,
I sat myself before her
like an empty coffee cup arrives.
I had come to solve
the mystery of our lives.
The waiter stood ready
and the cook was in the kitchen.
I awaited her order with great expectation.
Under her breath she purred,
"I'd like a kettle of stars."
She smiled and shrugged her shoulders,
and went on, "I'd like sunsets in crystal jars.
All my afternoons I'll have roasted in ovens;
The chilliness of my nights warmed in pots.
Beneath my bedroom blankets spread my legs;
then twist them tight and let me loose
spinning like a top into the Milky Ways;
there among the stars I'll fall asleep
to wake a thousand Christmas Eves of joy
my eyes spinning like a child's upon a toy."
I looked at the menu stunned.
"Waiter," she paused,
as she opened her hand exposing her claws,
her ring finger without a band,

voicing her aristocratic airs,
about liberal ethics and conservative affairs
both falling below her high flying philosophies;
then she purred beneath her breath,
as I tried not to look perplexed,
"I've changed my mind," she said,
"I'll have some tea instead."
I thought she'd want a house with a piano,
a dog, a picket fence, or romantic place to go.
But putting sunsets in a glass, . . .
my little restaurant I'd concocted
didn't have a pot of chilly evenings warmed,
or roasted afternoons, or Milky Ways,
or things to spin her legs into Christmas Eves
and other things ordered from her dreams.
I knew she was just speaking in metaphors;
but, also what her words were intended for.
Those things she wanted ordered up
were not on any menu I could concoct.
She was gracious and settled for
a tea bag, cup and saucer,
with two metal spoons of sugar
and hot water.
Lest my romantic notions be revealed
and on the restaurant floor all spilled
and the night brought to end.
I carried my heart away,
like an empty cup upon a tray.
'Twas a quaint restaurant in my mind
invented to ask her to live life with mine.
I wondered if one day, I might ask,
if she'd found the restaurant she'd sought;
or from the Milky Way she'd gotten back.

Her front porch was like an outdoor toilet
where careful words turned the handle
of our conversation's end to be flushed
down into that imaginary sewer pipe,
where one's romantic notions come to end.
I swirled from her life, down under ground,
into bigger and bigger sewer pipes
that ran unknown beneath the town.
I began to mix with the other turds
who'd lost their way that night.
We were all on our merry way
to the sewage treatment plant.
Laughter and music were in the pipes.
We were all a bunch of losers with our gripes.
Other, wiser turds than me made jokes
about what to do when we awoke.
The sewage water moved swift and sparkled
as if a kettle of stars had been poured
into the drain pipes.
Alas, her big words and cosmic dreams
snuffed out my hopes.
A diamond fell from my mind's box
melting thin for restaurant mops.

Opus on God and Monkey

The story swirls in the Milky Way
about when the monkey didn't know his place;
when he was a mere doodle in God's brain
and disobeyed God's order to stay in trees.
Angry, God crunched him up into a paper wad
and tossed him into outer space.
But, before giving the monkey a toss,
God broke the monkey's key to Eden's gate
and it spattered into a million fiery fish
that swam behind the monkey's face.
The fish on fire gave the monkey light
to glimpse the land from which he came.
Unlike God's other expulsions of life,
the monkey could apprehend his own demise.
So, while the fiery fish swam inside his brain
the monkey sang, danced, and talked insane.
He was haunted by his dream of Eden
and cravings to return to God's garden;
the place from where he began and came
and while he longed he danced and sang;
while the fiery fish swam inside his brain.
'Twas a ferocious aquarium
where the fiery fish did swim;
too dangerous for even God and angels
using heaven's nets to pull the fiery fish back in.

The tourist shops in heaven
put the monkey on display.
Where angelic patrons saw the fiery fish
behind the monkey's brain.
They asked God, "Why,
fiery fish swam behind the monkey's eyes?"
God gave them a nonchalant reply,
"The monkey is a piece of art.
made to understand its lot."
Angelic patrons fluttered away with awe
as they watched the monkey's life dust
stream across the universe.
God's angelic groupies took a moment
from their harps and songs;
they glanced down with amusement
to watch the monkey ride rockets
out of God's waste cans;
miles away from Eden's gates;
backwards falling out of gas;
tumbling back to earthly lands.
The Angels laughed at the monkey
as he tried wearing suits and ties;
trying to climb back into Eden's trees;
and scoffed at his scientific efforts to be
more than one of God's intended things.
Bored with the monkey's song and dance,
without a thought the angels went to flop
and wallow in the clouds.
God felt safe he did not have to negotiate
with the monkey for the key to Eden's Gate.
After all, the monkey had been a doodle
on a scrap of paper tossed from Eden's trees.
The key to Eden was a million fiery fish

swimming inside the monkey's brain;
a place too dangerous to hang out for Gods
and for the monkey too complicated to comprehend.
If the fish were yanked from the monkey's head
it would leave the monkey dead.
A piece of art with knowledge of it's own demise
would surely worry itself insane and to suicide.
So the monkey danced and sang;
while fiery fish swam inside his brain.
There must have been a night when God awoke
from a nightmare about the monkey and the key.
Dreaming of the monkey wearing shoes and clothes,
attending conferences, discussing the applied sciences,
looking for the key within their consciousness.
What if the monkey untied the knot,
and burst through Eden's gates?
Monkeys transformed into Gods!
Driving tanks and flying helicopters
bursting through heaven's clouds;
a monkey army of conquerors!
Parachuting fireworks into heaven
exploding in God's garden of perfection.
Blowing up Eden with a bang and a cry,
the feathers of God's groupies spiraling into the sky.
When the monkeys arrive in heaven
no thunder and lightning greets them in opposition.
They ask the shell shocked angels,
"Where is the artistic God we've heard about?"
They search for God under every rock.
With experiments and microscopes
they try to flush him out.
They search the clouds
and while they sack and plunder heaven of its prize

fish on fire swim behind their eyes.
The monkeys hunt for God exhausted,
in a quandary they debate
whether a God exists;
or was he simply asleep.
The monkey is forced to ask,
"Does an absent God have relevance?"
In absentia God is placed on trial
and charged with creating art
that could understand its lot.
A jury of monkeys with banana scepters
in their fists beating their hairy chests
makes conclusions of law and findings of fact
and orders up the ultimate judgment.
"Because monkeys by themselves can open Eden's door
there is no need for a heavenly doorman anymore.
From this day God and monkey are the same
and hereafter heaven will be in the Monkeys' name."
So it would be equality that ended God's long reign;
and monkeys were quick to claim heaven in their name.
From then on heaven was called the Land of Man
and the Gods of Monkeydom would rule the land.
Chips were hacked from God's abandoned throne;
carried back to earth from where the monkey'd come.
The chips were glued to trash cans, rocks and bone
They made a bridge to heaven,
and there they made a throne.
Monkeys came to heaven in buses, cabs and vans,
dividing heaven into political districts for elections
of congressmen, senators, presidents and kings.
God and his angels, dispersed and dispossessed;
no longer worshiped by the masses they were left
to fly about the heavens like lightning bugs to die

eaten by the fiery fish behind the monkey's eye.
It was frustration for the monkey; because,
he had failed to locate God.
He'd conquered Eden and become a deity;
he had left heaven burning, sacked, and robbed.
Yet, even with heaven's victory in his pockets,
he couldn't make footprints in the clouds.
Then God rolled over and shook his head;
woke up from his dream and laughed;
looked out his windows at the Gates of Eden
and saw no monkey armies in his path;
nothing to usurp his angels from their song;
looked at Gabriel's chest heaving up and down;
and felt protected by his terrible lips
and his hand that held the deadly horn.
Then God walked from inside his mansion
and stood on his front lawn,
paused and said with a mournful sigh,
"I wish I hadn't broke the key
behind the monkey's eye."

My mother's sister married a Lutheran minister. My Dad played the piano, and that meant he had to play the organ at church services. As a child I had to attend Sunday School, and listen to Uncle John's sermons. Uncle John gave hell fire and damnation sermons that rattled the walls

Ode to abandoned police station

I

Abandoned police station you sleep by tourist shops and city harbor.
  Strange there is nothing to extol your past grandeur.
What untold stories of derring-do behind your walls must hide?
  A metal fence with bars imprisons your history from the curious eye.
Your main archway has no plaque or flag that stories patrolmen brave and bold;
Who with bullets and smoking pistols brought bad men into custody;
  To give the pursuit of justice their lives and blood.
You trumpeted the academy lesson about protecting life and property.
  It was you who stood against evil in the cold night and offered protection.
    Now your hollow skeleton lies abandoned and forgotten.

II

An orphan son who once wore badge and gun stands outside the station wall.
  He wonders what terrible monster could have caused his father's fall.
After all, the purpose of the police station was to protect property and life.
  He gently places his hand on the station's wall as if to feel a pulse,
or perform an autopsy; then in dismay he pulls his hand away
to ask, "What is a police station anyway?"
  At best a house of shepherds with guns protecting rights and pursuing wrongs.
At worst a box of tin stars that turn a few patrolmen into momentary gods
  and for a few moments outside the court police become the hands of fate
    fixing wrongs and rights in the darkness of the night

III

Like a fallen god of yore abandoned without praise.
    What powerful demonic event could have stolen your pride?
What colossal event occurred that you now rest unadorned?
    It was from your stomach long ago patrolmen went to the streets;
With guns, clubs and handcuffs each to cast shadows of giants.
What of those patrolmen, now forgotten orphans every one?
    You were the father of patrolmen who honored right over wrong.
Their muscle, blood and thought were your soul and rule.
    How could the city fathers leave you without acclaim?
        The day your doors were closed perhaps they were afraid.

IV

Since the first Roman Centurion with spear and shield took a complaint
    From a citizen of Rome about the emperor's law being broken
Human nature has remained the same.
    Surrounded by the smell of sulfur and blue-pink flares;
Before a patrolman decides to make an arrest; before a detective
Begins to lift a latent print with charcoal-dust and tape; or in a cushy office
    in the sky the lonely district attorney deigns to prosecute;
none can but think about the options in their heart
    of what or who would benefit
        from their decision to charge or not.

Ode to abandoned police station

V

Behind your cold walls the careers of honest men were lost.
　　Good men accused of dispensing justice outside the court;
not to scare the criminals, but set a price on broken silence by police.
　　Patrolmen and chiefs faced accusations of scandal and crime.
Turf wars and station politics caused investigations to implode and slide.
On graduation day recruits threw away the pursuit of misdemeanor and felony.
　　The reign of self-investigation was ushered in with a siren crying emergency.
Public relations hacks, sycophants and chiefs scrambled over station walls
　　to find safer positions in other towns, to look back with red faces
　　　　to watch the defenseless eaten by the monster in the station.

VI

Your story is of loyal men and ambitious chiefs.
　　A tale of protecting life and property wrapped in circumstances
of trust and power that eventually forces each patrolman to ask,
　　"Where shall I place my heart?"
In the hands of brother cops who cover my back with pistols cocked!
In books of law and men in robes that seek justice in this world;
　　Or justice of the ultimate kind in the worship of divine.
Some find the answer in the law, others in their god, alas some exchange
　　Their soul and silence for a part; or like the orphan son,
　　　　turn in their badge and gun.

VII

Without a celebration of great deeds, without a stone or plaque,

    Without a speech that lauds the dead to insure no questions asked;

This is the way great police stations are retired;

    One day the doors are closed and a demon comes to guard;

To guard against the brave deeds of lawmen springing forth;

The whisper in the monster's breath takes the form of simple truth:

    "When silence is exchanged for promotion and reward,

now and then, instead of law silence is enforced."

    Best step soft about this building's vacant rooms

        and not disturb ghosts of past investigations closed.

It was 1973, my last year as a police officer and under the dome light of my patrol car I was studying for law school. Until then when on patrol my mind was on catching crooks, but law school forced me to study for my classes. The upper ups had put me on a beat where there was not much crime; I didn't know if they wanted me to pass the bar or bore me to death on a quiet beat until I quit. I would find a place to hide so I could study law and keep my sergeant from finding me. I felt guilty. But, trying to keep from being seen while studying for school worked out well. I hid in several locations that were difficult to find. Ironically my hiding spots overlooked the same routes robbers used to make their getaways. Other officers asked how I managed to be on top of the robberies. I knew my luck would not last forever. The arrests were flukes. Yet, there was sort of an unexpected consequence logic as to how it worked out well for me. After I proved to myself I could make good grades in law school, I took my police retirement and finished school.

Studying law under the dim dome light of the patrol car made me feel insignificant and tiny because the worldly books of law, arguments of great dead men hundreds of years before and real life conflicts going on outside my windows was a thrilling time in my life. The goal of passing the California State Bar and writing my books, and to me, my precious poetry, seemed far away.

The Ghost of Judy Mae Hess

Tricky Dick sat in the Oval Office.
Everywhere he looked
he saw an Indian Princess.
Outside the White House gate;
in the Rose Garden when it was late.
He slammed his fist upon his desk.
Damned Watergate and John Dean!
He wondered from where the protestors came
as they shook images of effigy
and chanted outside the White House lawn.
They carried placards that libeled his name.
Tricky Dick thought Deep-throat was to blame.
But it was really the ghost of Judy Mae Hess.
A girl on a puppet show, a long dead actress;
It was she that led the protest.

Let me tell you the story of Judy Mae,
about young love, violence and fame.
She was the hostess of a children's puppet show;
and in 1953, the producers let her go.
Her crime was stealing the hearts of little boys
and becoming more popular than the show's toys.
Children were told she'd gone to Indian Heaven,
a Happy Hunting Ground where there was fun.
Mothers in kitchens fixing dinners

saw their children pointing fingers at TV sets.
Parents called TV stations to learn
the titles of the players behind the screen;
writers, directors, sponsors and producers.
The first TV kids learned who pulled the strings.
Some of us looked for her the rest of our lives.
We were haunted for years by her disappearance.
I found out one day by accident,
in an old obituary in a magazine.
The Indian Princess in the TV set
had the real name of Judy Mae Hess.
She had been fired which was what we thought.
But she made a comeback with Elvis
in the movie Jail House Rock.
Her skyrocket to success was cut short.
Judy Mae Hess, every little boy's Princess,
died in a car crash in Rock River, Wyoming.
The obituary failed to mention
her absence from a puppet show in 1953,
was the most romantic event of the 20th Century.
Who could have predicted or known
one day in the future her fans would return
to confront a larger puppet show.

the firefly ring

(Legend says, if you kill a firefly the dying glow creates a window for an
evil thing to look at you. Blind to the human heart evil cannot hear its beat;
except, through the window of the dying firefly's light.)

Once upon a time two poor lovers walked
among fireflies in the night.
They were afraid and running from their past.
Too poor to buy wedding rings,
her coin-less pockets and his dusty suit;
They dreamed of greater things
than walking in the night.
Within the cathedral of the heavens
they caught their breath and prayed for castles
in the sky and in desperation caught
a firefly and rubbed its yellow tail-light
into a wedding ring around her finger.
Rubbed it into a yellow-ember
that pulsated on her finger.
They walked together in the night
her finger pulsating a yellow-green.
Two lovers part of the night's scene
among a million flashing golden lights
clustered over hills and dales of flashing quilts.
They walked toward a starry castle in the sky.
Their hearts began to sigh.
The earth was light beneath their feet.

They began to float upward in the air

between the ice white moon and stars

above the golden flashing blanket

that spread like an ocean on the planet.

The evil thing awoke and opened its eye to hear

a curious note that throbbed about her finger.

It watched the dancing lovers

twirl and spin toward the stars.

Through the glow of her ring that throbbed

the evil thing could see her heart and blood.

She tried to hide her hand in her dress,

but the ember's light came through the cloth.

Then she covered her pocket with his hand

and they fell from heaven to their end.

I wrote the *firefly ring* in 1960, at La Jolla High School, in San Diego, California; but the idea began in Ohio, when I was fourteen, on a muggy spring night in our New Concord, Ohio, backyard– it was the Spring of 1959, I was swinging a baseball bat at fireflies and splattering them into fireworks. Climbing a ladder out of the fireflies on to the top of our house was like coming out of a swimming pool that covered the earth composed of tiny golden flashing lights. The fireflies hung over the land in all directions at a height of two stories. From the top of our house a quilted ocean of golden dots spread over the farmlands. The night sky was coal black, a snow moon and a billion tiny stars as white as snow flakes formed a magical canopy over the flickering golden ocean.

I'd been told the reason people rub the firefly's glowing yellow on their fingers was because they couldn't afford wedding rings. On top of the house that night in Ohio, I got the idea for this poem and it was written for Mr. William McCann's English Class at La Jolla High School, in California. I was 16, and I never turned it in.

Being little more than a C student, I had to petition to get into McCann's English Class. That semester McCann read an essay I wrote to the whole class. My essay that semester was the only one he read. My classmates went on to become extraordinary people. In back of me, Tom Oliphant, famous Boston Globe Columnist, and to my immediate left Garth Murphy, famous historical novelist. Murphy, after surfing in the morning would come to class with his hair wet from the Pacific Ocean, wearing sandals and shorts. Oliphant would have grownup conversations with McCann over my shoulder. La Jolla high school was a change from the tough farm boys in New Concord, Ohio, who came to school with cow shit on their boots; and, the hard working blue collar boys in West Virginia. I was blessed to grow up at 2 & 3 Qt. Mi. Creek, West Virginia, and New Concord, Ohio, then move to California.

Old Joe's dirt

Old Joe's City no longer exists.
Covered in the mud of politics.
In heaven, maybe hell, somewhere
Old Joe is rocking in his chair.
Whether with fire or feathers he's sure
to be building insurrections;
organizing lesser devils against Satan,
or fallen angels against gods in heaven.
The Russian people are not drowned by politics.
The story of the battle over Old Joe's City
is handed down one generation to the next.
Whether Old Joe looks from heaven's clouds
or from under hell's icy waters,
he sees his masterpiece of defiance.
A portrait of free will painted with the lives
of Old Joe's sons and daughters;
who declined to dance the "goose -step"
with a foreign army on their land.
With bloody fingers, rocks, and bullets
children used the colors of their lives
and giving up their spirits in cold mud
smote the Nazis in their tanks;
the blitzkrieg in its tracks was stopped.
Old Joe gave precious time to allies
Winston, Charles, and Dwight,

to think, to plan, to attack.
If man is the creator's art,
then blood is the paint,
and mud the parchment
on which freewill is brushed.
Don't look puzzled when I remove mud
from beside the road to Stalingrad;
to cradle through Berlin across an ocean
to the other side of the world;
to rest in the land of the American.
To put Old Joe's dirt in a tin can;
place it on a front porch in Michigan,
to grow Forget-Me-Nots,
with roots of dynamite and sweet bouquets
of gun shots from far away.

    I was preparing final argument in the "Russian Boat Case," at the time, the largest government cocaine seizure in the history of the United States. Representing a young Ukranian sailor who was on the ship with a crew of about 12 others.

    During my research for my final argument I channeled the battle of Stalingrad and wanted to use it in some way in argument to the jury to bond our two countries in that these defendants were citizens of the Ukraine/ Russia on trial in the American Justice system. The Cold War had left a lot of scars and I was looking for common ground. I knew the American jurors would give these young men some reasonable doubt but wanted to set the stage. So when I was preparing my argument which I do throughout the case I started working on the idea of Russia and Germany fighting it out at the City of Stalingrad and how important that battle was for us Americans. Anyway, I was surrounded by exceptional defense attorneys and we got good results.

Jewish Girls and the Devil's
Fiddle Strings

Oh, Jewish girls, Oh, Jewish girls, I love them;
but I'll never get to heaven for what they've done.
Oh, Jewish girls, Oh, Jewish girls, I love them;
but I'll never get to heaven when kingdom come.

You see, my heartstrings are playing music for the devil;
my heartstrings are on the devil's fiddle he plays in hell.
The devil plays tortured music for the sinners on his fiddle
as they dance amongst the fires, the screams and yells.

Oh, Jewish girls anesthetize the goy boys with their kiss
then pull the goy boys' heartstrings from their chests.
They deposit heart strings in New York bank accounts
then sell them to the red-horned devil at discount.

When the goy boy gets up his chest feels hollow.
But, he doesn't know his heartstrings are in hell.
He hears strange music that he wants to follow
that comes from up behind and makes him yell.

Jewish girls stole my heartstrings and my heaven.
For the money they could not help themselves.
Maybe they thought they would be forgiven
amongst the devil's fires, screams and yells.

Jewish girls don't believe in hell or heaven.
They will never have to listen to the devil's song.
Although they keep his fiddlestick in business,
They don't have time to hear the devil's wrongs.

Oh Jewish girls, Oh Jewish girls, I love you,
as the Devil's music pulls me towards his hole.
I sit and listen to the devil's music like a fool,
and you will never feel my pain inside your soul.

I walk about the world singing my sad songs
'cause my girlfriends picked my heartstrings clean.
They don't care how the devil's fiddle sounds
as I roast upon the devil's fires and scream.

Oh Jewish girls. Oh Jewish girls. I love them.
But, they only care for heartstrings they can sell.
Because of them I'll never go to heaven
'cause my heartstrings play the music down in hell.

Linda Opie's Eyes

I

In the high school lunch line
we'd almost stand beside.
There I'd stand all smitten
and peek at Linda Opie's eyes.
She was unaware of the risk I took;
as with pennies from my heart
I purchased cakes and milk.
Our lives and eyes never met.
Linda never turned to greet
is my great regret.

II

About the color gray in Linda Opie's eyes,
there were poems I didn't write but tried.
I struggled to say her eyes were gray
like the windy sea on a rough day.
My efforts were crumpled into paper wads,
then tossed into a thousand waste cans
that became the graveyards
of my unfinished rhymes.
I prayed to describe her eyes of gray
that never once glanced back my way.

III

For words to rhyme about her eyes
I searched years and months;
but never found the words in rhyme
to express the way I felt.
One day I ventured back
to that empty high school path;
where we purchased cakes and milk
to find some parts of me I'd left.
Suddenly I lost my breath.
I stood there quite in shock!

IV

Before me stood the very words
for so very long I'd sought.
The words for my rhyme's end
I'd finally found, I thought.
They still stood at attention
waiting for Linda to turn and look.
The words were very stoic;
they still hoped to get a view.
They stood there very quiet,
a sad and lonely crew.

V

I exclaimed, "Hurray! At last!"
I'd found the words to end my rhyme;
but my words spoke,
"We are the words you left behind.
You should have let us leave your lips
when your heart was young.
In wait we spent our lives
inside your silent tongue.
We never got the chance
to keep your heart unbroken."

VI

They said, "Leave us alone!
Without a look from Linda Opie
there is no ending to your poem.
Perhaps she'll walk by one day
and see us all in line,
ask if they still sell cake
and we'll try to catch her eye."
I wanted to punctuate their loyalty
with commas and parenthesis
my rhyme at last in harmony.

VII

I turned about to think
on what my words had said;
and when back I turned to look,
they lay in line all dead.
Their lives spent in wait to speak;
now they'd left without a peep.
I gently picked them up,
their deaths were in my hands;
watched them through my fingers slip
beneath my unfinished lines.

VIII

To those who read this rhyme,
no ending was written by my hand.
I'm told in the reader's mind
words appear I never wrote;
between unfinished lines
gray eyes cavort and flirt.
Linda leans out from inside my verse
and the reader's lips are kissed;
then she turns and smiles;
an experience I've always missed.

What is the weather?

What is the weather where you are?
Are there glass buildings and fast, fancy cars,
dancing cows and green pastures of dollars;
ice cream forests surrounding a mountain peak;
conversations with elves and laughter's delight;
a night sky with white stars dancing bright;
the night itself dancing in a black suit
the moon a carnation on the night's chest
begging you jump out of your dress.

In the mornings do you get up from your slumber
and look for coffee and cold pizza in the refrigerator?
What is the weather, what is the weather?
Here are a bunch of warm words out of clouds
friendly warm rain drops falling to ground;
remnants of thunderstorms that fell us apart;
Oh hell, you know the ones that broke my heart.

Dinner at the Ritz

I saved my money to go to the Ritz
where waiters wore fancy suits.
Finger bowls were scattered around
like Beverly Hills swimming pools.
During the meal I was jostled
by another eater's fork
searching inside my plate
for whatever it did want.
I watched my meal split and twist
to avoid the fork's sharp taste
and thought it queer,
me sitting there
at the table of the great.
You see it was a meal
where you ate up your life.
I looked around
wondering how I'd survived
all the forks and all the knifes
when like a lettuce bug
I'd run wild in salads all my lives.
Zeus' daughter sat across my plate.
She was no ordinary date.
I sat there staring at her face.
I sat there eating up my fate,
evaluating what to save,

what to spite; what part of me
to hide before I spoke to Calliope.
How ancient were her lips,
her eyes, her nose so coldly wise;
but, it was her indifference
that held me hypnotized.
As she ate and drank
with her steady gaze,
she embraced me like
midnight's frozen haze.
What she was I did not know;
but, self-absorbed I'd lived
and laughed between her arms;
and hadn't thought to understand
the where-with-all about her charms.
She invited me to an ancient auditorium;
where, "I'd find the audience
as interesting as the play."
Then teased me with a smile
and made me wonder what to say.
She talked of eternal life,
death, and the boring lives of gods.
After dinner we took a walk
to the back stage of the stars.
Where she asked,
"What if in the middle of your life
you were given another script, . . .
that whatever, and wherever
your life was you would start it up again?"
That instead of the person you were out to live,
a new role of who and what would metamorphosis.
"What audience is this again?"
I asked.

She handed me a script
and I gave it a quick read.
I'd play the director of a play who wept
because his heroine and gal in real life
with the hero of the show had slept.
I'm out of leading men," I'd say,
"The hero's been shot in the head.
The detective says, "I'm the prime suspect
and the heroine is crying in my bed."
I wrung my hands and asked,
myself could I learn the lines.
Better yet could I improvise?
I stood behind the curtain
guessing when to start.
Calliope left my side
to sit with critics in the dark.
She said I knew all of them,
and they all of me;
and she would sit and chat
with them throughout eternity.
I studied my lines for my entrance
and when the curtain finally rose
I looked in back my eyes
to see an empty house of ghosts.
There was no laughter or applause.
The audience unseen, and hushed.
It was the audience of the great back stage;
with no applause or outrage;
where limelight splashed on empty seats;
phrases bounced on cerebral cushions
and gentle came to rest inside the heart.
I shut my eyes and looked, but, . . .
no faces looked me back;

no traces of those who came and went.
An auditorium of empty seats.
I was director of a theater of dreams.
The audience, writer and actor in my fantasies;
a living auditorium composed of those
once alive and now trapped inside my flesh.
An audience of the ghosts of dead men
running through my blood;
sitting in the auditorium behind my eyes.
I, the actor-writer-director all in one.
Yet, with all of them inside,
I felt alone;
all of us the same, same, same person.
Calliope came smiling and sat down,
"It's your turn."
"For what?" "I asked.
She said, "To entertain the dead,
to have some fun;
for all those spirits once alive and gone;
for those watching who cannot speak;
watching, silent with clenched teeth;
watching, watching, watching, . . .
in the back, back, back, back seat.

Target Practice for the Gods

As we whisked him off to jail,
I looked at him through the rear view mirror
while my partner told him he was evil.
"It's liquor that turns you into a devil!"
She teased him, . . . and she made me smile.
But, I told her,
"You're just going to get him riled."
The old man in the prowl car cage
shouted and ranted with rage.
His blue eyes bulged with a white glaze.
"You think you're gods,
But, without bullets you are duds."
My partner and I laughed.
He would talk then he would babble,
but all the while he cursed and spit
at the back of my partner's seat.
So I got the prowl car going fast
then hit the brake just like that,
and just as he was about to spit—
the car came to an abrupt stop
that pushed him forward to crack
his angry cursing head into the metal rack
that separates front seat from the back.
"How is he doing there in back?" I asked,
"Did he pass the screen test?"

My partner turned and took a look.
"Looks like on the old man's head, . . .
He's got a little bump."
"Is he still spitting, or did he pass the test?"
I asked.
"I think he passed," my partner said,
"but, he just might need to take the test again
'cause he still looks pissed and mean."

Happy tourists in the Grant Hotel
unaware of the commotion in our squad car
looked down beyond their finger bowls
through the windows at our moving blur
on Broadway's wet dark streets;
where white steam through manhole covers shot
with a hiss to hang in cloudy pockets
through which our patrol car burst
with a silent pop.

The old drunk began to rant and rave,
"You think you are gods," he exclaimed,
"But, where are your followers?
. . . Where are your disciples?
Without guns and bullets you're worthless.
Do you know where your disciples are?"
My partner told him, "No, why don't
you tell me?"
"Your disciples are the bullets that sleep
in your revolver chamber.
They worship you in closed eyed prayer."
The old drunk's words were full of crazy logic.
My partner looked at him and said, "You are an idiot."

The words in his babble just popped out
like scrambled pictures in television static.

He continued on the same theme.
"A circumstance inside your mortal eye
will select your disciple's beginnings and endings.
Let them out to crash fast upon life's road
and die, never to know who, what or why they are."
The old drunk was on his way to jail.
His voice was full of alcohol and ale.

So when he talked about gods and bullets
I didn't give a piss.
But as we splashed through the ghost clouds,
I chewed the old drunk's words inside my soul.
My job was driving heaven's bullet
through the lowest clouds on earth.
Were his words an omen?
A warning of things to come?
But my thought was forgotten.
There were arrest reports to be done.
The old drunk was booked.
The jail door slammed shut.
Again our patrol car had an empty stomach.
We drove to "Johnny's Restaurant,"
and I began to write the arrest report.
Our ears were tuned to "Station A,"
the police radio frequency.
My partner sipped her coffee
and wrote her 153.
The radio popped and sighed.
Then the dead air that hangs empty
when there is no radio traffic came alive.

The sleeping sack of air awoke and cracked.
Our squad car was assigned--
a strange call and my partner raised one eye.
". . . a man under a house with a Bible and a gun."
At the destination we arrived and found
a prowler crawled beneath a woman's house
and now he was praying beneath her floor.
She told us first she noticed noises in the night.
She drew her skirt about her waist so tight;
and with her teary face appeared distraught;
telling us she was hearing someone at prayer
beneath her wooden floor, and the scare
was she thought the prayer was being sent to her.
"There is a prowler beneath my wooden floor.
I can hear him making prayer. I'm scared,
and I can't sleep or go anywhere.
Can you get him out from under there?"
A neighbor volunteered he'd seen the prowler
crawl through a hole and under.
He said the prowler was armed
with a Bible and a gun.
My partner asked,
"Should we try to coax him out,
or just leave him to decide?"
"Whatever he might be beneath her floor,
he thinks the lady is a god.
The sounds of his prayer
from underneath the floor
come up and scare her to the core.
The lady wants him gone."
So we entered through a hole in the cellar wall.
Upon our stomachs we begin to crawl.
We broke cobwebs and chased spiders through
the underbelly of the house.

We made our way to where
a face looked back at us with beads of sweat
that sparkled in the darkness behind the flying dust.
In a dim glow of flash light
the prowler clutched his bible and his gun and asked,
"From where have you come?"
"From above the wooden ceiling," I replied.
He whispers to us,
"Do you hear the steps of the goddess?
She walks about in her evening gown.
She does not hear the prayers that I've spoken.
I speak soft when I pray to my love above.
Sometimes she steps so close above my head.
I could reach up through the wooden floor and grab her foot.
But I cannot penetrate the wooden floor.
I don't think she listens to my prayer.
Do you think she knows the agony I bear?
The life I lead beneath her heaven?
Does she understand the darkness and my pain?
Should I pray louder?
Should I shoot my gun through the wooden ceiling
to grab her attention?
I pray, and pray, but mostly I just listen
to the soft thunder of her steps above my head.
My partner asks, "Do we want to play along with this
until we know just how gone he is?
Because," she whispers, "I'm already convinced
he is psychologically unfit."
I speak to him softly, "We have come from above
the wooden ceiling. The woman that lives up there,
she doesn't want you under her floor."
He gives us a strange look and cries back, "My love,
my goddess does not want my prayer.
My goddess does not want me here anymore.

Doesn't want my worship beneath her floor."
My partner tells him, "Your prayer
makes her a little nervous."
She doesn't know who you are."
His head shakes and he mumbles,
"No, No, I can't take this."
He looks back and forth
at his gun then at us.
I tell him, "She doesn't want you to fire
your gun into the wooden sky.
You have gotten her attention.
Now she wants you to go away.
Suddenly, we heard footsteps above our head.
They gave the man a start.
He dropped his gun into the dirt.
Then he grabbed for his gun in the dim light
while shadows went berzerk
breaking and jumping in the dark
as if to point the gun at us—
or just to pick the gun up from the dust.
In a fraction of an instant
six lead-faced sailors were let loose.
Lightning and thunder struck beneath the house.
Gone, all gone each bullet's life spent
so quick and fast.
Only for a moment their lives last.
Beneath the house a man lay dead.
A flashlight, Bible, gun and blood.
From beneath the wooden floor we emerged.
Shaking we walked up to the lady's door
and simply said, "He will not bother you anymore."
I sit silent and await the coroner.
Detectives take empty shells from our guns
and toss each spent cartridge into an envelope.

Spent bullets are replaced with fresh,
and unspent bullets sit ready to explode.
There is an emptiness in and out.
We need to be told we were right.
We wait and listen to the dead air in the night.
My partner's eyes look at me up tight;
and sure we followed the rules and we're right.
But, I can't help but ask,
"Am I in a target practice for the gods;
being shot, and shot again in preparation
for a cataclysmic fracas; or something less;
a bullet in the rifle of a drunk and reckless god;
who, swaggering in his back yard,
shoots to wound the stars and moon
beyond his comprehension?

Listen to the police frequency called station "A"
slowly winding out her song,
picking and choosing partners in the sky,
and winding hearts and muscle into destiny.
She deals a hand of cards to each,
a game of poker in the night;
where the ante is a patrolman's fate
and winning hand a life.
Station "A" draw tight
your strings about my partners in the night.
We sit silent in our squad cars and await
the next call to be directed where to go.
I travel where I'm aimed,
I go where I am told.
Yet, while toward the mark I speed,
I wonder about being bold,
and where and how I shall explode.

In the 1960s the old Grant Hotel, on Broadway in downtown San Diego, in the evenings would release its scalding water into the drain pipes, the steam would shoot up into the outside streets as puffy white clouds, and cars on the street would plough through them. Doesn't happen anymore. Somebody must have gone down under the streets and fixed the hot water pipes. These days, I can sit in my law office and look out the window where the clouds on Broadway used to puff up, and I'd drive through them with my patrol car.

If there was a God and he could hear our prayers, and we were right under heaven's clouds; and, the prayers were interfering with the angel's songs and harps, would God send his cops down to tell us to move along? The poem is fiction. No one was shot. I did, on one occasion, go under a house and talk a guy with a Bible and gun out. Sitting in your patrol car waiting for a call that will put your life on the line, and blindly going into danger. The nature of being routinely sent to danger made not just me, but everyone I worked around contemplate their existence and purpose.

Love Songs Past

When she left she took more than my heart.
So alone I felt I could not talk.

I didn't talk for over a year.
Just listened to songs remembering her.

Then one day I spoke my first words.
Everyone was surprised at what they heard.

I could only repeat the romantic words
from old love songs when I was hers.

The songs I embraced as strong as could be
their lyrics and rhythm became part of me.

Now I am trapped in words of fantasy.
I cannot talk in reality.

Everybody tries to talk to me.
Most give up cause I'm sorta crazy.

That is how I'm gettin' along.
Just repeatin' the words of old love songs.

I'm a hopeless romantic in the real world trapped.
By phrases and words from love songs past.

If not in my songs it's just not important.
So, just let me be 'cause my mind is locked.

Don't ask me why my life is this way.
This is the way she left me to stay.

Don't ask me why my life is this way.
This is the way she left me to stay.

The Measured Man

I am a measured man.
My spontaneity has been calendared, and parsed.
My erotic future neatly divided into plots.
She's made my love a string of obligations
to be performed exactly and in certain ways,
at particular times and on specific days.
My love has been tightly scheduled;
on her moderated, calendar's page.
Through thousands of my own capitulations
like lawn grass my manhood has been mowed.
By all of this my passion has evolved, . . .
to a measured, scheduled love.
She wears a calendar necklace,
a symbol of my obligations, and her dominance;
with her gentle intimidating persuasions.
I sleep on the couch collared like a dog
to avoid her sharp tongue, "You snore."
She's calendared my passions into pieces
like a jig saw puzzle she has put together.
I am something that she organizes
like the furniture she moves upon the floor.
Oh, god, she is a bag of bitches.

I didn't think passion could be organized.
The problem is I've been surprised!
She has me organized, . . .
into moderated fits of love and kindness;
trained me with rewards and punishments;
and now, sometimes I'm like a dog surprised
with how well she's got me satisfied.

A guy out for a look

Hey, I'm just a guy that wants to see New York
I'm just a guy, I'm just a guy out for a look.
I want to see the Great White Way,
attend a real Broadway Play,
Salute the Lady with the Flame!
Then I'll sit at Harold Square
and hear Gershwin everywhere;
At ground zero give a prayer
against oppressors everywhere.
Hey, I'm just a guy, I'm just a guy
that wants to see where King Kong climbed.
Just a guy that wants to see New York.
I'm just a guy out for a look.
At Harold Square I'll stir a drink
with Reggie's straw.
I'll read the New York Times
and give regards to all.
I'll take the walk in Central Park,
buy the Brooklyn Bridge for sport,
and when I've seen enough and through
After fireworks and kissing you.
I'll hop a jet to Arkansas;
where I'll brag I saw it all.

Looking for flying reindeer

It's still early in December,
the clouds are full of colors;
but, . . . there are no reindeer,
no Santa Clauses.
Everyone is so polite.
Everyone is so nice.
At Christmas it's like, . . .
Angels are watching us.
In the air Santa Claus and reindeer
are circling in his sleigh, invisible.
In the streets and stores there's laughter.
It's such a struggle. It's such a struggle
You say Santa Clause is an old fool.
He delivers presents every year;
but, he doesn't seem to know
that some of us don't care.
I'm looking out the window,
looking deep into the sky
looking for flying reindeer, . . .
and perhaps Santa flying by.
I guess these days that's queer.
But, I don't want to hear
about reindeer that don't fly.
About how you don't love me
because it will make me cry.
When your in love, anything can fly.

Anything and everything else is a lie.
I'll just sit beneath my tree
looking for Santa Claus
to save me from the meanies
you've spread around my house.
Take your humbug and condescending remarks
about my views on reindeer and Santa Claus.
Put them in a bag and get out of my house.
Besides, it's still early in December,
the clouds are full of colors;
but, . . . there are no reindeer,
no Santa Clauses.
I'm going to sit by my tree,
looking out the windows,
for flying reindeer to save me.
I don't want to hear
about reindeer that can't fly;
about how you don't believe in Santa Claus,
because he's not alive.

Kathy again

Another dream about Kathy again.
She was playing a piano
with a delightful song.
She was plucking sweet notes
about loves gone wrong.
She was in a hilltop house
by a winding road;
and the music trickled out
all over the world.
Her eyes were light green
with a trace of pink,
and freckles slid down
her nose and her cheek.
Off the livingroom left
was an all man quartet;
whose soft strums nourished
the invited guests.
Her family and friends
moved within and about;
and for a moment,
I was in her house.
Just for a second,
a ghost from her past;
then the wind pushed
and my dream didn't last.

The ghost in my pencil point

There is a ghost in my pencil point.
The thought that squirted out,
perhaps I didn't want.
The word that made me blink;
that I didn't think.
The word that jumped
without a thought.
The ghost in my pencil point.
If the ghost gives me displeasure,
I'll perform an exorcism with an erasure.
If the ghost brings me praise,
I'll claim the word is mine and plagiarize.

Columbus

I named my kite Columbus
    and with a tail of words
let it loose in search of sense
    in countless other worlds.
Printed on its paper wings
    the phrase, "In Search of Sense."
It flew beyond the clouds
    into emptiness.
Columbus' taut string snapped
    went limp against my hand;
then it disappeared
    its string falling to the land.
One day in the Land of Emptiness
    an explorer will find its wings
crumpled and directionless
    in great vast empty things.
Like eagle-eyed Americus
    high in Maria's nest
looking for a new world,
    he'll discover my Columbus.
His crew out loud will laugh
    at my kite's wiggling string
and unanswered questions
    about from where it came.
The Captain will toy the string
    that hangs from rescued kite;

contemplate the message left,
    "In Search of Sense" the plight.
He'll ponder where the string snapped,
    then let Columbus drift
back into the emptiness;
    where there is no sextant,
no latitude, or longitude
    to determine its location.
Where thoughts push the sails
    in this world;
no ups and downs and no directions;
where thoughts are wind, and minds are wings.
Where all of us have broken strings.

Nails & Wings

I've got one hand in heaven,
    and one hand in hell.
I've got a problem
    I've got to tell.
I just can't decide
    on which to turn loose
'cause both of these
    bastards dance like a goose.
One hand is red, with
    gold rings and white nails.
The other is white
    like the wings of angels.
With both of them pullin'
    at the same time,
sometimes I feel
    like I'm losing my mind!

                Nails and Angels, Rings and Wings.
                Who says the Devil and God
                don't sit down, to talk over things?

I hear the devil's dreams
    running like a river fast;
I feel the breeze of angels
    soft upon my back.

Drunk on the Devil's water,
    and full of heaven's holy prayer
I believe I'll dance forever,
    Angels singing everywhere.

In my heart nails and wings are fighting
    for the last taste of my soul.
Outside the chapel angels smiling
    through the chapel window.

I saw a cup of coffin nails
    resting on the floor.
The angels loudly laughing
    as the preacher closed the door.

The preacher told the congregation
    where the soul was going to go
and to make some prayers to the gone
    so the devil would not know.

All the parish bowed their heads,
    and prayed God save their souls.
Never thinking God and devil
    decide on where they'll go.

The Other Fisherman

At the beginning of the shift
the lineup Sergeant read the list
of evil deeds to keep us current
about suspects we would hunt.

While my partner and I stare
with one eye open at the floor,
a Priest leads us in a prayer
like we were in Sunday School chairs.

Then the Sergeant hands us a sheet
containing suspects on our beat.
We had all the bullets we could shoot,
gasoline in the squad car tank,
and in our trunk a hundred flares.
So we began the hunt,
for the most dangerous
    . . . animal on earth.

While on patrol,
our squad car spins around.
The police station became a temple
and a vast circle of water the ground.
Our patrol car became a boat; and,
our guns and clubs into fishing poles spiral;
with hooks and lines they stretch for a mile.

A sea of moving visions in a whirl
surrounds our tiny boat in this strange world.

My partner is now a Priest.
He tears a page from his testament
and places it upon a line and hook,
then it drops into the visions from our boat.

One Patrolman and one priest,
silent with our poles we sit and think.
What lies port, aft, and beneath,
as visions slide beneath our feet?

The page of Bible wiggles on the hook.

Down deep a crook,
sniffs and nudges at the bait;
which he takes with one great shake.
Pulled aboard with one quick yank;
dripping with a brutal look;
each tooth razor sharp,
he bites the Priest's oar
that falls apart.

The Priest's Cross of Jesus
I use to club, and beat the crook
into the hull where he struggles
until the hook and page of Bible are spit
away from his wicked smile.

The visions began to come
over the little boat's side,
and the Priest is swept overboard;
while puddles in the boat began to rise.

The crook, I pushed back into the wild
where he smiled and slid
beneath the sea of images.

Upon return to the Police Temple, . . .
there was a message someone left
upon the temple door that flashed
in multi-colored neon light:

       "... Priests for souls do fish,
          policemen for flesh;
          neither know whose catch
          serves an absent father best ..."

On the beach the Priest
had come to rest upon the sand.
I found a note
clutched within his hand.

"Beware!" it said.

       "... A fisherman named fate
        also floats about and drops bait.
        Who knows who will be the fish
        and who its bride."

I paused, and for a moment thought
how difficult to separate
the role of man from that of fate.
Each Patrolman and each Priest,
their catch of flesh and souls they moor
at their respective temple door;
while fate's catch drifts to wash ashore.

Squad cars with a thousand eyes
and ears on radios
are spread across the city like a net.
Images drift by my prowl car windows
in a city evening sprinkled in black night.
Our patrol car has an empty stomach,

as my partner drives us through
the sprinkled lights of dark.
My private thoughts are like gunshots!
Yet, they make no sound.
As to some distant altercation I am bound.

    I wrote The Other Fisherman sometime between 1967, and 1973, under the dome light of my patrol car. Years later, pulled it out of one of my poetry boxes. It occurred cops hunt people for punishment, priests hunt souls for repentance, and forgiveness; and, there is this indifferent thing called fate out there hunting us all, making no distinction between our personal ideas of good and evil. Although fate is indifferent and without morals; fate, while we debate and fight among ourselves over who is most good and evil, fate claims all of us. Not to say our discussion about good and evil is wrong; but fate closes everyone's door. Doesn't give a damned about what we do or think. We have enemies among ourselves, crooks and sinners; and then, we have this other indifferent reality that gets all of us.

My true love

I've written some words I don't understand.
I'm looking for someone to lend me a hand.
I wonder if these words will ever be sung.
They are all about love.
They are all about love.

I've forgotten more rhymes than I've written.
I've written more words than I know.
I keep coming back to the beginning;
But, I really don't know where to go.
But, I really don't know where to go.

I've kissed more lips than I should have.
I've wanted to kiss more than those.
But, I don't think I've ever kissed my true love.
I've always just let them go.
I've always Just let them go.

My Explosive Heart

From birth my heart was filled and mixed
with sulfur, charcoal and potassium nitrate.
I could not away from myself run.
I was the bomb. I was the bomb.
All my life I'd been waiting for the explosion.
Waiting for the one.
The one who would someday come.
The one who would ignite.
The one who would begin my life.
But true love never came.
The absence of true love caused my heart to ache.
I'm ashamed to say how many came and went.
So many hearts I lost, let's just say,
I just lost count.
I didn't mean to disappoint.
It was not I could not love or like.
It was just that only true love could ignite.
But true love never came.
Oh, there were proms and dates;
but I never heard guns and rockets
that others fell in love and heard;
and I began to wonder whether I ever would.
So my explosive heart I hid.
Told myself the powder in my heart was wet.
So, I hid my explosive heart
and there in the dark it sat.

It sat so long that I forgot.
I told myself there was no thing as love.
Not such a thing as romance.
That the words, "A true love would come."
Were words only for the dumb.
After years of building walls and rock,
I'd completely given up, and then forgot
that true love could exist.
So, when I took her to the moving picture
there was no thought of true love
as her hand I gave a touch.
Just popcorn to eat and munch
and a moving picture there to watch.
But she charmed me in an inadvertent way
by sticking her face into the popcorn bag
to eat the popcorn like a horse.
Then a chat that was innocuous;
and I knew, I really knew, just like that;
although I was charmed and impressed,
for me, the time for one true love had passed.
From birth, my heart was filled and mixed
with sulfur, charcoal and potassium nitrate.
When my heart finally did explode
love for me would be here and there
to cherish for as long as love would care.

The double alibi defense

(Letter from a man accused of robbery in San Diego,
to the Missouri District Attorney, Carrie Mc Cartney,
asking not to be extradited)

Dear Carrie McCartney:
Please let me be.
Missouri does not need to extradite me.
It's in San Diego, I have to stay
and show the jury I should be free.
So, Carrie McCartney, don't extradite me
back to Missouri where I shouldn't be.
My attorney, Charlie Guthrie, tells me
he can tell the jury about my story;
how I was charged wrongfully
for committing a crime I didn't do.
Now I'm locked in a jail in San Diego.
So, Carrie McCartney, please let me be.
Missouri does not need to extradite me.
It's in San Diego, I have to stay
to show a jury that I should be free.
Attorney Guthrie will tell my story
in as how I couldn't be guilty.
It won't be that overused excuse
I was in the wrong place at the wrong time.
It will be a defense that will twist the mind.
You see, I have the defense of a double alibi!
Attorney Guthrie will tell my tale

and the jury will agree I shouldn't be in jail.
After deliberating a short spell
they'll proudly vote to acquit and set me free.
Can't you just believe what I say?

Don't ask the Missouri cops to take me away.
Don't extradite me in handcuffs and chains
to spend my life in Missouri the rest of my days.
Carrie McCartney, before you extradite me
let my attorney, Charlie Guthrie,
tell the San Diego Jury my double alibi story.
In San Diego, he'll argue it was true
I committed a robbery, but not in San Diego.
He'll argue I committed the robbery in Missouri;
and a guy can't be in two places at the same time
in Missouri and California committing a crime.
So, Carrie McCartney, could you help me out
by sending the victim in Missouri south?
Down to San Diego for my reasonable doubt;
I'm sure the man in Missouri will identify me
as the one who robbed him in Missouri, you see?
My Attorney Charlie Guthrie says the robbery
victim in Missouri is my alibi for the San Diego crime;
after all, a jury won't believe I could commit a robbery
in Missouri and California at the same time.
Carrie McCartney, I promise you
when my trial in San Diego is all the way through;
and the famous Charlie Guthrie gets me off;
I'm buying a ticket on a Greyhound bus.
My destination will be Missouri and because I'm not a crook;
I'm putting you on notice that I'm buying another ticket
for that teller of tales and explainer of crime
my Attorney Charlie Guthrie, who's now a friend of mine.
Oh, I'll also be bringing the San Diego victim;

the one that told the jury I robbed him.
The victim in San Diego, that testified against me;
the same victim the San Diego jury didn't believe.
Why in Missouri he'll take the oath and be confident
when he says he was robbed in San Diego by me.
He'll explain to your Missouri jury that is picked;
I couldn't have been in Missouri and robbing someone
when I was in San Diego robbing him with a gun!
My attorney Charlie Guthrie calls this a double alibi.
Why I'm as certain to be found not "Not Guilty"
as, "Heads," on a two-headed dime.

CHARLES N. GUTHRIE

The Shepherd's Eye

It just comes one day by surprise.
You look at yourself and realize,
you never really looked before.
You turn around to comb your hair,
in the mirror looking there,
the person you knew as you is gone.
Someone that wasn't there before
looks back with your face and hair.
It's hard to say how it comes about;
Perhaps a cryptic note hung upon a door
about a flat tire on a car--
for some reason a person is no more.
That person you used to know as you
unties the noose and raises the chair.
What you were before you wore
the badge and gun has passed you by.
You see the world through the shepherd's eye.
The way you change the way you look to you
and how the world changes to your view.
Pull your gun and hold the grip;
careful with the trigger pull so light.
Watch the suspect's hands move,
and be prepared to shoot.
What you were before you wore the badge
and gun has passed you by.
Walking the line between evil and divine

you learn the taste of evil and its smell.
In order to survive you break the rules
and you look for evil's footprint even
in that part of your heart you call your own.
It comes one day by complete surprise,
drawn to evil are your eyes,
and nothing you will ever do,
and nothing you will ever try
will return you to that innocent guy.

Elegy to Hank

Hey Hank, where did you go?
The last time I saw you,
you were playing ball with Bo.
You dunked the ball
and the crowd roared.
The game was over.

The announcer speechless.
Play was stopped.
Referee whistles wouldn't go off.
There was silence in the crowd.
Referee's didn't know on who to call the foul.
Gone were cheers and pomp.
The pep band music stopped.
No play sent in by the coach.
The crowd stared at the clock.
The players on the floor walked off.

Hey Hank, where are you are?
Up there in heaven, . . . what's the score?
Did you jump to heaven on that last dunk?
Does St. Peter have a hoop and court?
Does everyone have wings and play the sport?
Hey Hank, is it against the rules to fly?
Is there a three point line, . . .
and a buzzer beater shot?

Hey Hank, when you can fly,
are you allowed to dunk?
When you got there,
did the Angels make you a star?
Do gods and angels cheer?
Do crowds in heaven roar?
Do you still wear jersey 44?

Do the Angels play on the hard wood?
Or, do gods and angels play ball in the clouds?
Hey Hank, in heaven is there an out of bounds?
And again I've got to ask, when everyone has wings is it against the rules to
walk?
Have you learned to play the harp?
At the games in heaven do the clouds roll and rock?
Does Gabriel blow his horn?
Do you play the Devils, and if you do, . . .
who keeps the score?
Does thunder and lightning strike
while the game is carried on.

Hey, Hank where are you are?
You left us in the crowd's roar.
You left your heart upon the floor.
You proved a shooting star
can fall to heaven from the earth.

I suppose, when you left,
the angels saw you coming like
a three point shot was took.
Did you get points for making it
through St. Peter's Gate?

Elegy to Hank

You showed us all what we suspected.
There is a spirit at play in the game---
A spirit only those that play so hard
they could die can see!
There is someone with us out there,
on the court, above the net, and in the crowd.

Something, or someone else among us
when we play the sport out loud.
You can call the spirit God or fate, or
some might call it luck.
But, there is another player out there
playing with us on the court.

And, yes, the crowd can feel it,
you don't have to be a jock.
It's like a witches' brew, and in most games
you can feel it before the game is through.
Just for the hell of it, I call the spirit Hank.
But, I really don't know,
it could just as well be Mike.

What he's playing for we can't figure out.
But, sometimes you play with him,
and sometimes you play without.
He's out there on the court;
but you can't see what he's about.
He doesn't catch the ball or shoot;
but he's everywhere and not.

With a strong spirit,
and afraid the game is lost,
and when your pounding heart
does not care if you live or not.

Sometimes at the foul shot line
you can look into that no man's land;
and embrace the spirits in your head.
Sometimes, not always, but sometimes
you can feel your spirits
dancing to the pounding of your heart,
and that's when you know the spirit
or something else is with you on the court.
There is no other feeling like it
that let's you know you'll make the shot.

The pounding in my heart
tells me I'm playing ball with Hank.
So Hank, did St. Peter give a reason for taking you away?
Did God need the strongest man on earth in a pickup game.
Do they play basketball in heaven?
Do you still leave the gym late?
We miss you here on earth;
but you showed us heaven's not that far away, . . .

So Hank, if you're at the foul shot line,
and you decide to shoot the ball with your left hand;
does the spirit on the court guide your mind?

In the middle of the hectic game.
The calm of the free throw lane.
In those moments looking
into the empty key, that for the moment
is a no man's land, you see;
and before you shoot the ball;
go through that old routine,
before you aim, bounce the ball,
feel its weight, and measure in your mind

the median and the mean;
then try to place the ball through a steel ring.

There is that moment when,
the ball travels from finger tips to rim;
where something else is in the picture
between your effort and the win.
Somewhere between the downward arc
and the ending of the shot;
before the swish, the careening role,
or the rattle of the ball, . . .
Just for an instant there is a moment lost—
something in the unseen world
decides whether it's made or not.
Then the swish, or the reverberation
of the metal of the rim,
and then the re-bounders jump and bump
when the ball does not go in;
or the referee will hand the ball back
from the magic place it came;
to be taken out again, and again in the game.

There is a movement in the game,
a back and forth of wills,
and in that mix there is a spirit
that moves, and sometimes stands still.
Two teams of wills that flow with each unfolding against the other on
the court;
but we all know there is something else out there moving in the sport.

I hear the bounce and ping of a basketball in an empty gym.
I look around and no one's there except cracks and pings.
Empty bleachers and metal chairs that echo in the empty air.
Hey Hank, is that you, in here with me, come to play once more?

After you made that last dunk shot,
you jumped to heaven from earth.
I'm out here by myself with a ball and hoop
playing with the ghosts.

There is a spirit out here on the empty court.
A feeling something beside myself
is outside of me, and everywhere; yet,
not exactly someone else.
I Don't know what to call the presence
because it leaves my mind blank;
but, I'd just as well believe it's Hank.

The Studebaker

I came among the congregation
to stand and pray on the cemetery lawn.
I was a child, come to pay homage
to ancestors that had come and gone.
The loved that walked before I was born;
but, they were still in the conversation.
Songs were sung and prayers read.
Sacrificed flowers placed on graves.
With a sore neck from a bowed head
and bored with songs and prayers,
I walked away into the graves.
Got lost and became afraid.
When I found my way back
my family had completely left.
My family's dead flowers sprawled
over the cemetery graves.
I saw the Studebaker that brought me;
it would stop then it would blow its horn.
Someone called my name
into the stretching shadows of the gone.
The sun lowered itself into the earth
and white clouds turned red rust.
I heard a final honk outside the gate;
a final call for me to come;
but, I could not help myself;
and hid among the shadows and the stones.

I watched the setting sun;
watched the shadows stretch to dark,
   found a tombstone that was warm,
where I placed my head for night.
   I spent the night among the spirits;
heard angels singing, saw devils dance and kick,
   goblin shadows digging in the cemetery crust.
In the morning I was found walking all alone;
   and I ran out of the tombstones
to hugs and kisses headed home.
   In the Studebaker back seat,
I saw wide-eyed faces in the front.
   They looked back concerned
and asked if I'd been afraid.
   I told them I'd had time to think,
if one day I'd come forever back;
   back to where I spent the night;
back to the tombstones
   where from inside the cemetery gate
I'd never be allowed to leave.
   But, to myself I knew I would be back one day,
and I'd never walk away.
   There would be no search party,
no Studebaker full of wide-eyes
   that would come to call my name.
No honking horn, or torches in the night.
   I would not be hiding among tombstones
to come running back to life.
   Friends would come and share last tears;
then they'd say a prayer and leave me there.

Back in West Virginia, and Ohio, at least when I lived there, country people, my people, would go to church on Sunday, and visit their ancestors and bring flowers to their gravesite. When I was about eight years old I walked away from one of those visits and was lost for about half an hour. It was a graveyard south of St. Albans, in West Virginia, off the great Kanawha River. I just made up the overnight thing. My parents would never have left me over night. But, even for a few minutes lost in a cemetery, what else are you going to think about but goblins? I was in fact found by my dad and family driving our old Studebaker around the cemetery honking its horn, and there were loved ones with wide-eyes asking questions in the front seat. I was scared and came running out of the stones.

CHARLES N. GUTHRIE

superpower of enough

There is a superpower everyone can touch.
One we can all possess.
A superpower that's all over earth.
A power hard to see because it's inside of us.
Some have it and some don't;
but, we almost all have some of it
because the power is so close.
Not easily recognized because it's so disguised;
but, if you want, you can grab it with your mind.
You have to understand it exists
between, "No thanks," . . and . . "Too Much!"
In other words the superpower
is knowing when to say, "Enough!"
Anyone can say "No!" but what's the point of that?
When you hurt you know you've had too much.
The power is knowing when to say, "Enough!"
before you hurt, and have to say, "Too Much!"

The Sorcerer Celeste

What circumstances
driven by Satan's Devils - - -
drunk on expectations
of an Angel's kiss;
bump their red horns
into their burning stomachs,
their white eyes shining
in the morning mist.
Why its purpose is for
cradling the attentions
of the Sorcerer Celeste.
Who with her spell, she stole
the hearts of Demons while
they beat within their chests.
Demons wandered outside her castle.
They searched blindly for their hearts.
While Celeste sat on her royal pillows
throwing laughter at the stars.
Her laughter drained and filled the moat
that ran beside her castle walls - - -
The demons kept on coming to slip
into the laughter and dissolve.
But, Celeste was unhappy with a sky
full of blinking stars.
A heaven that had more stars
than she demon hearts!

More stars than she could ever steal - - -
Jealous of the stars that twinkled,
she conjured a spell to break the tranquil
of the night.
A spell to make the stars stop blinking,
and instead of their twinkle,
she would make them squeal.
When it came about,
it was such a horrid sight!
A heaven full of squealing stars was not right.
The Demons cared no more
for their hearts and stopped their search.
The stars became a nuisance
and everyone pissed off.
So, Celeste reconsidered and let
the stars blink again - - - went back
to stealing Demon hearts
and never messed with stars again.

ghosts in me

"There are ghosts in me!"
the young man screamed.
"They have the same mouth and eyes
as me, but there are ghosts in me.
The crazy is they all agree.
They all agree on what to say
and what they see;
But, I tell you there are ghosts in me."

The place on the door

The place on the door that marked my height.
It burned up with the house one dark night.
The fire could be felt in a dream on the coast,
when I rolled over and awoke.

I survive without you

Oh honey, I survive without you,
don't need you, not at all,
I moved on in an instant after
you were gone.

But sometimes, not all the time,
for no reason at all, I wonder
where you are, how you are doing
and so on.

Maybe my big kiss off was not as permanent
as I thought, cause every now and then,
gosh darn, I think of you when I ought not.

Do you think of whether I have thoughts
of you, and if my feelings once were true?

Oh honey, my life is run for my own fun,
and you are hardly on my mind;
but yesterday the thought of you
came up to visit me, and your memory
stayed all night.

I know you're just remembrance
of a romance I once had;
but now I'm thinking what to do, 'cause
you're sleeping in my bed;
even though I know you're not alive,
and just a ghost inside my head.

I know you're just remembrance
of a romance I once had;
but now I'm thinking what to do, 'cause
you're sleeping in my bed;
even though I know you're not alive,
and just a ghost inside my head.

The girl with shotgun eyes

On a walk I passed a girl
whose eyes grabbed mine
like shotgun shells.
Those rifled eyes
got the drop on me,
and when my hands went up
a host of melodies went free.
Sweet thoughts that licked love's wounds,
I didn't want to lose.
Love's spirits inside my mind;
all creations of my own design;
forces that ruled my world,
that long prowled my insides
were pushed out by her rifled eyes.
Loves that lived inside my head
like shadows from my insides
now flickered on the outsides.
No heroic effort on my part
to pull them back inside my heart.

The one who set my loves on fire,
was a girl with shotgun eyes;
whom I thought about,
that passed me on the street;
I took a look and she at me.
A girl I'll never know or meet
disarmed me of what haunted me.
She set my ghosts of love on fire,
and burned them up in front of me.

Master of my Pants

When I get up
the first thing I do
is put on my pants
but not like you.
I don't put my pants on
by following the rules,
one leg at a time,
like other guys do.
I take a jump in the air
and at the highest point,
put both feet in my pants
and land all at once.
At the end of my day,
I take a great leap in the air,
yank my pants off
and end my day there.
The point of this rhyme
is I'm master of my pants
from the start of the day
until the last.
It's a secret I've kept about myself.
I don't put my pants on like everyone else.

The Author

Charles N. Guthrie grew up at 2 & 3 Qt. Mi. Ck., West Virginia, and New Concord, Ohio, moved to California when he was 15, graduated from San Diego State University and holds BS and MS degrees in Criminal Justice Administration. He received his Doctorate in Law

Photo by James D. Weiner, Asterelics

from Thomas Jefferson School of Law. He was a City of San Diego police officer for 7 years, and left the department when an acting sergeant to complete law school. He attended McKinley Junior High, St. Albans, Junior High, and Dupont High School in West Virginia. In New Concord, Ohio, he attended New Concord High School (now John Glenn), and moving to California graduated from La Jolla High School. Other books authored are *The Palace Guard*, a fairy tale for policemen, *Neptune's Laughter*, an epic poem about the legendary surfer Charles "Butch" VanArtsdalen, and a textbook, published by Harcourt Brace, *Security Guard, Powers to Arrest*. His Masters Thesis on police response to domestic disputes written at San Diego State University was used to fashion California's current domestic dispute laws. He practices law in San Diego, California, and has done so for over 35 years. He is the creator of *The Grammar Policeman*, a series of grammar workbooks for police studying for the sergeant's exam.

CPSIA information can be obtained
at www.ICGtesting.com
Printed in the USA
BVHW021436130623
665881BV00010B/273